KINGFISHER 🐦 REFERENCE

CHILDREN'S CONCISE
ATLAS
OF THE WORLD

Edited by Jane Olliver

Kingfisher Books

Kingfisher Books,
Grisewood & Dempsey Ltd,
Elsley House,
24–30 Great Titchfield Street,
London W1P 7AD

This revised and updated Concise edition published
in 1992 by Kingfisher Books.
Originally published in 1987 by Kingfisher Books as
The Kingfisher Children's World Atlas, which was a
revised and expanded edition of *First Picture Atlas*
published in 1980 by Kingfisher Books.
Reprinted in 1993

British Library Cataloguing-in-Publication Data
A catalogue record for this book is available
from the British Library

ISBN 0 86272 967 X

Concise edition edited by Andrea Moran with
assistance from Janice Lacock
Designed by Heather Gough and Terry Jeavons
Flags supplied by Lovell Johns, Oxford.
Authenticated by the Flag Research Center,
Winchester, Mass. 01890 USA
Printed in Hong Kong by South China Printing Co
(1988) Ltd

Contents

Countries of the World	4
The Continents	6
The British Isles	8
Netherlands, Belgium and Luxembourg	10
Scandinavia and Finland	12
France	14
Spain and Portugal	16
Germany, Switzerland and Austria	18
Central and Eastern Europe	20
Balkans and Romania	22
Italy and its Neighbours	24
Russia and its Neighbours	26
Southwest Asia	28
India and its Neighbours	30
China and its Neighbours	32
Japan	34
Southeast Asia	36
Canada	38
USA	40
Mexico, the Caribbean and Central America	44
The Andean Countries	46
Brazil and its Neighbours	48
Argentina and its Neighbours	50
North Africa	52
West Africa	54
Central and East Africa	56
Southern Africa	58
Australia	60
New Zealand and the Pacific	62
The Arctic and the Antarctic	64
Facts and Figures	66
Index	75

Countries of the World

Greenland

ICELAND

NORV

UNITED KINGDOM

Alaska

IRELAND

CANADA

FRAN

SPAIN

UNITED STATES
OF AMERICA

PORTUGAL

MOROCCO

ALGE

TROPIC OF CANCER

MEXICO

BAHAMAS

MAURITANIA

MALI

CUBA

56 DOMINICA
ST LUCIA
BARBADOS

53 54 55

46
47 48
49 50

26

27
28   29

32

30
31

33

51 52

VENEZUELA

57

COLOMBIA

58
59 60

ECUADOR

EQUATOR

PERU

BRAZIL

BOLIVIA

TROPIC OF CAPRICORN

PARAGUAY

URUGUAY

CHILE ARGENTINA

Falkland Islands

0   3000 kms

0   2000 miles

4

FINLAND
ESTONIA
LATVIA
LITHUANIA
LAND
RUSSIA
A
B
C
D
0
ROMANIA
BULGARIA
12
GREECE
TURKEY
E
F
G
L
I
K
H
J
MONGOLIA
NORTH KOREA
SOUTH KOREA
JAPAN
CHINA
13 16
14
15 17
IRAQ
IRAN
AFGHAN-ISTAN
PAKISTAN
NEPAL
22
18
19 QATAR
YA
EGYPT
SAUDI ARABIA
20
OMAN
23
INDIA
MYANMAR
TAIWAN
HONG KONG
LAOS
THAILAND
24 VIETNAM
PHILIPPINES
AD
SUDAN
21
41
SOMALIA
ETHIOPIA
MALDIVE ISLANDS
SRI LANKA
BRUNEI
MALAYSIA
SINGAPORE
34
38
ZAIRE
39
40
KENYA
TANZANIA
SEYCHELLES
INDONESIA
PAPUA NEW GUINEA
SOLOMON ISLANDS
OLA
ZAMBIA
42
MADAGASCAR
43
BOTSWANA MOZAMBIQUE
IBIA
44
45
SOUTH AFRICA
VANUATU
NEW CALEDONIA
AUSTRALIA
NEW ZEALAND

A	RUSSIA
B	BYELORUSSIA
C	UKRAINE
D	MOLDAVIA
E	GEORGIA
F	ARMENIA
G	AZERBAIJAN
H	TURKMENISTAN
I	UZBEKISTAN
J	TADZHIKISTAN
K	KHIRGHIZIA
L	KAZAKHSTAN

1 DENMARK	21 YEMEN	41 DJIBOUTI
2 NETHERLANDS	22 BHUTAN	42 MALAWI
3 BELGIUM	23 BANGLADESH	43 ZIMBABWE
4 LUXEMBOURG	24 CAMBODIA	44 SWAZILAND
5 GERMANY	25 TUNISIA	45 LESOTHO
6 ITALY	26 SENEGAL	46 BELIZE
7 SWITZERLAND	27 GAMBIA	47 GUATEMALA
8 AUSTRIA	28 GUINEA-BISSAU	48 HONDURAS
9 CZECHOSLOVAKIA	29 GUINEA	49 EL SALVADOR
10 HUNGARY	30 SIERRA LEONE	50 NICARAGUA
11 YUGOSLAVIA	31 LIBERIA	51 COSTA RICA
12 ALBANIA	32 BURKINA FASO	52 PANAMA
13 CYPRUS	33 TOGO	53 JAMAICA
14 LEBANON	34 CENTRAL AFRICAN REPUBLIC	54 HAITI
15 ISRAEL	35 EQUATORIAL GUINEA	55 DOMINICAN REPUBLIC
16 SYRIA	36 GABON	56 PUERTO RICO
17 JORDAN	37 CAMEROON	57 TRINIDAD AND TOBAGO
18 KUWAIT	38 UGANDA	58 GUYANA
19 BAHRAIN	39 RWANDA	59 SURINAM
20 UNITED ARAB EMIRATES	40 BURUNDI	60 FRENCH GUIANA

The Continents

NORTH AMERICA

SOUTH AMERICA

FACTS ABOUT EUROPE
(Including the former USSR)

Area:
Europe apart from the former USSR is 4,874,040 square kilometres; **the former USSR** is 22,402,200 square kilometres.

Population:
Europe, 501,000,000
USSR, 288,000,000
Number of countries: 35
Largest country: Russia, which is part of the Commonwealth of Independent States. Russia is in Europe and Asia.
Smallest country: Vatican City
Highest mountain:
Communism Peak in the Pamir Mountains; 7495 metres.
Largest lake: The Caspian Sea, 371,000 square kilometres.
Longest rivers: The Ob-Irtysh river is 5410 kilometres.

FACTS ABOUT NORTH & CENTRAL AMERICA

Area: 24,249,000 square kilometres.
Population: 425,498,000
Number of countries: 22
Largest country: Canada
Smallest country: St. Kitts-Nevis
Highest mountain: Mount McKinley, 6194 metres.
Largest lake: Lake Superior, 82,103 square kilometres.
Longest river: Mississippi-Missouri-Red Rock (USA) 5970 kilometres.

FACTS ABOUT SOUTH AMERICA

Area: 17,600,000 square kilometres.
Population: 297,780,000
Number of countries: 12
Largest country: Brazil
Smallest country: French Guiana
Highest mountain: Mount Aconcagua in Argentina is 6960 metres high.
Largest lake: Lake Titicaca in Bolivia and Peru, 8300 square kilometres.
Longest river: The Amazon in Peru and Brazil is 6440 kilometres.

| 0 | | 3000 kms |
| 0 | | 2000 miles |

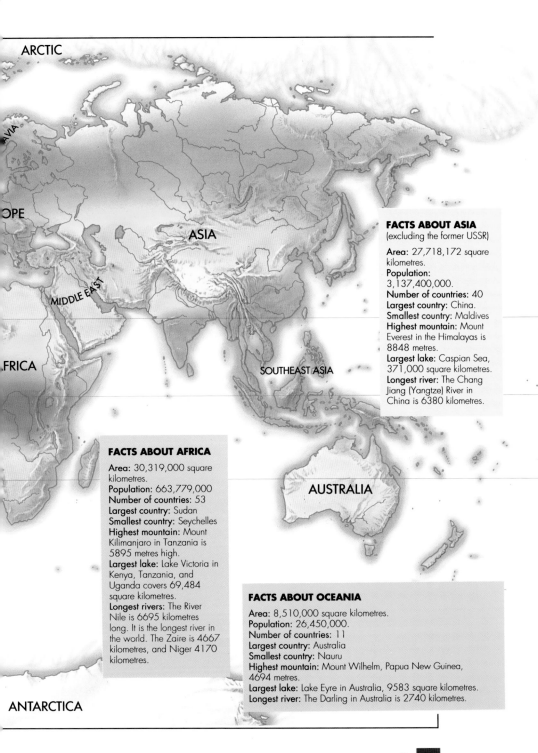

ARCTIC

AVA

OPE

ASIA

MIDDLE EAST

FRICA

SOUTHEAST ASIA

AUSTRALIA

ANTARCTICA

FACTS ABOUT ASIA
(excluding the former USSR)

Area: 27,718,172 square kilometres.
Population: 3,137,400,000.
Number of countries: 40
Largest country: China.
Smallest country: Maldives
Highest mountain: Mount Everest in the Himalayas is 8848 metres.
Largest lake: Caspian Sea, 371,000 square kilometres.
Longest river: The Chang Jiang (Yangtze) River in China is 6380 kilometres.

FACTS ABOUT AFRICA

Area: 30,319,000 square kilometres.
Population: 663,779,000
Number of countries: 53
Largest country: Sudan
Smallest country: Seychelles
Highest mountain: Mount Kilimanjaro in Tanzania is 5895 metres high.
Largest lake: Lake Victoria in Kenya, Tanzania, and Uganda covers 69,484 square kilometres.
Longest rivers: The River Nile is 6695 kilometres long. It is the longest river in the world. The Zaire is 4667 kilometres, and Niger 4170 kilometres.

FACTS ABOUT OCEANIA

Area: 8,510,000 square kilometres.
Population: 26,450,000.
Number of countries: 11
Largest country: Australia
Smallest country: Nauru
Highest mountain: Mount Wilhelm, Papua New Guinea, 4694 metres.
Largest lake: Lake Eyre in Australia, 9583 square kilometres.
Longest river: The Darling in Australia is 2740 kilometres.

The British Isles

Ireland

United Kingdom

The British Isles is made up of two countries: the United Kingdom (UK) and the Republic of Ireland. The UK consists of Great Britain (England, Wales and Scotland) and Northern Ireland. Many people call the UK simply Britain. The Republic of Ireland or Eire was once part of the UK. But in 1921 it became a separate country.

A moist climate makes Britain and the Republic of Ireland ideal for farming. But in Britain one-third of the food must still be imported, or bought from other countries. The farms are too small to feed the large population.

Industry is very important in Britain. For every person working on the land, there are ten people living and working in cities. Britain pays for the food it imports by providing services and selling oil to other countries.

ABOVE: *Traditional fishing villages like this one in County Kerry are typical of the coastline of the Republic of Ireland.*

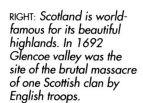

RIGHT: *Scotland is world-famous for its beautiful highlands. In 1692 Glencoe valley was the site of the brutal massacre of one Scottish clan by English troops.*

ORKNEY
ISLANDS • Kirkwall

SHETLAND
ISLANDS

HEBRIDES

North West Highlands

• Inverness

Loch Ness

Ben Nevis
1347m ▲

Grampians

R. Dee

• Aberdeen

R. Tay

Tay

Oban

Loch
Lomond

Perth

• Dundee

• Dunfermline

NORTH SEA

0   200 kms
0   100 miles

Glasgow •
R.
Clyde

• Edinburgh

• Ayr

SCOTLAND

R. Tyne

• Newcastle
upon Tyne

○ Londonderry

NORTHERN
IRELAND • Belfast

Sligo •

Lake
District

R. Eden

Pennines

• Middlesborough

ISLE OF
MAN

• York

Lough
Mask

Central Plains

• Galway

Blackpool ○

Bradford
•

• Leeds • Hull

IRISH SEA

Liverpool
•

Manchester
•

Lough
Derg

R. Shannon

• Dublin

R. Barrow

Wicklow
Mts

▲ Snowdon
1086m

Stoke-on-Trent •

• Sheffield

R. Trent

ENGLAND

Nottingham
•

The
Fens

Norwich
•

REPUBLIC OF
IRELAND (EIRE)

• Waterford

WALES

Cambrian Mts

Birmingham
•

Leicester
•

R. Ouse

Great
Yarmouth

• Cork

• Fishguard

R. Severn

Coventry
•

Cotswolds

Cambridge
•

Ipswich
•

Swansea •

Oxford
•

Chiltern
Hills

London
•

Canterbury
•

Cardiff •

○ Bristol • Bath

Reading
•

R. Thames

North Downs

Dover

Exmoor

R. Avon

Southampton
•

South Downs

Brighton
•

Exeter •

• Portsmouth

Dartmoor

Bournemouth •

Isle of
Wight

CHANNEL
ISLANDS

• Plymouth

Land's End ○ Penzance

ENGLISH CHANNEL

ISLES OF SCILLY

Netherlands, Belgium and Luxembourg

Belgium

Luxembourg

Netherlands

The Netherlands, Belgium and Luxembourg are known as the Low Countries because much of the land is flat and below sea level. In the Netherlands high dykes, or sea walls, have been built around low-lying lands, which are called polders. Nearly a quarter of the Netherland's land has been reclaimed from the sea in this way.

The Low Countries have a combined population of around 25 million. This makes them the most densely populated group of countries in Europe. They are also wealthy countries. Most people work in offices and factories, often in textile and electrical

companies. Others work on the land. The farms are small but are modern and well-equipped. Dutch farmers grow either flowers or vegetables or keep cows. Oil and natural gas are important resources in the Netherlands, and there are also large iron and steel mills in Belgium and Luxembourg.

ABOVE: *The Atomium is in Brussels, the capital of Belgium. The design is based on the structure of an iron crystal, magnified 165 billion times.*

RIGHT: *Amsterdam is the capital of the Netherlands. The city is criss-crossed by more than 100 canals. Many of them are lined with tall, narrow buildings.*

FRISIAN ISLANDS

• Groningen

Waddenzee

0 _____ 200 kms
0 _____ 100 miles

NORTH SEA

IJsselmeer

R. IJssel

Haarlem •

⊡ Amsterdam

• Apeldoorn

• Enschede

NETHERLANDS

Leiden •

• Utrecht

The Hague •

R. Lek

R. Rhine

• Arnhem

Rotterdam •

R. Waal

• Dordrecht

Nijmegen •

R. Maas

Breda •

• Tilburg

• Eindhoven

Ostend ○

• Antwerp

GERMANY

Bruges •

Ghent •

BELGIUM

R. Lys

• Maastricht

• Brussels

R. Schelde

R. Meuse

• Liege

○ Mons

Namur •

Charleroi •

FRANCE

Ardennes

LUXEMBOURG

• Luxembourg

Scandinavia and Finland

Denmark

Finland

Iceland

Norway

Sweden

Thousands of years ago, Scandinavia was covered with ice sheets and glaciers. These cut deep fiords into the coastline and formed many lakes and islands. Iceland is the most northern country in Europe. It still has many snowfields. It is also dotted with hot springs, geysers and over 100 volcanoes.

ABOVE: *Most of the agriculture in Norway takes place in the southern lowlands. Goats are prized for their cheese, which is a speciality of the region.*

Most Scandinavians enjoy a high standard of living. Sweden is the largest and richest of the countries. Over half the Swedish people live in modern cities, such as Stockholm and Gotenborg. Many earn their living by manufacturing paper, furniture and other wood products, as Sweden, Norway and Finland have large areas of forest. Sweden also exports minerals such as iron ore and zinc.

Scandinavia's coastal waters teem with fish. Fishermen, mainly from Iceland and Norway, catch large quantities of cod and herring which are then canned or frozen in factories.

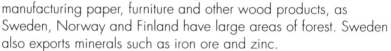

Denmark is made up of the peninsula of Jutland and about 600 small islands. Greenland, the second largest island in the world, is also a province of Denmark, but has its own government. Dairy farming is important in Denmark. One-fifth of the people are farmers, and they use the latest machinery and farming methods.

LEFT: *Over half of Sweden's land is covered in forests. When the trees are felled, the logs are transported by river to coastal sawmills.*

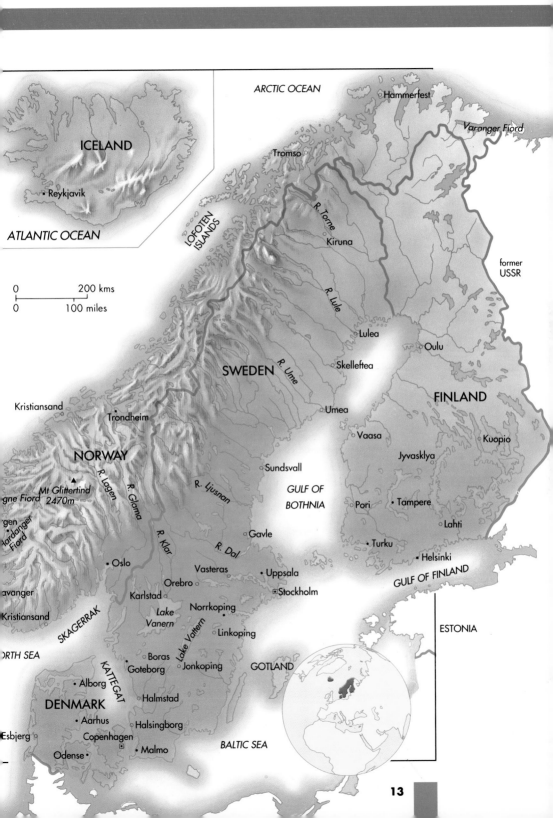

ARCTIC OCEAN

Hammerfest

Varanger Fiord

ICELAND

Tromso

ATLANTIC OCEAN

· Reykjavik

LOFOTEN ISLANDS

R. Torne

Kiruna

former USSR

| 0 | | 200 kms |
| 0 | | 100 miles |

R. Lule

Lulea

Oulu

SWEDEN

R. Ume

Skelleftea

FINLAND

Kristiansand

Trondheim

Umea

Vaasa

Kuopio

NORWAY

Mt Glittertind 2470m

gne Fiord

R. Lagen

R. Glama

R. Ljusnan

Sundsvall

GULF OF
BOTHNIA

Jyvasklya

Pori

· Tampere

Lahti

gen
ardanger
Fiord

· Oslo

R. Klar

R. Dal

Gavle

Turku

· Helsinki

avanger

Vasteras

· Uppsala

GULF OF FINLAND

Kristiansand

Orebro ·

Karlstad

Norrkoping

⊡Stockholm

SKAGERRAK

Lake
Vanern

Lake Vattern

Linkoping

ESTONIA

ORTH SEA

Boras

Goteborg

Jonkoping

GOTLAND

KATTEGAT

· Alborg

Halmstad

DENMARK

· Aarhus

Halsingborg

Esbjerg

Copenhagen

· Malmo

BALTIC SEA

Odense ·

France

France is the largest country in Europe, except for Russia. Along most of its borders there are mountain ranges. The Jura Mountains separate France from Switzerland, the Pyrenees separate it from Spain, and the Vosges separate France partly from Germany. The Alps border France with Italy and contain Mont Blanc, which at 4807 metres is the highest peak in France.

Although many French people work in factories, farming is very important. The warm climate and rich soil help farmers to grow cereals, fruit and sugar-beet. Grapes, used for making wine, are grown in most regions. But the main grapevine growing areas are in Bordeaux, Burgundy and Champagne. Dairy farming is also

France

Monaco

ABOVE: *The imposing church of Sacre Coeur is one of Paris' best known landmarks. It stands on a hill at Montmartre, an area famous for the many artists who have lived and worked there.*

important and over 300 different cheeses are made.

Paris, Lyon and Marseille are the main cities in France. Painters and writers from all over the world have lived in Paris. Many tourists go there today to see its historic buildings, which include the Louvre, the Notre Dame Cathedral and the Eiffel Tower.

LEFT: *France is famous for the good quality wines it produces. Vineyards can be found throughout the country, but especially in the drier southern regions which have the best soils for grapes.*

GREAT BRITAIN

NORTH
SEA

Dunkerque
Calais
Boulogne

BELGIUM

Roubaix
Lille

Valenciennes

Douai

ENGLISH CHANNEL

Dieppe
Amiens
R. Somme

LUXEM-
BOURG

CHANNEL
ISLANDS

Cherbourg

Le Havre

Rouen

R.Oise

Reims

Metz

R. Seine

R. Marne

Nancy

Caen

Paris

R. Meuse

Strasbourg

Brest

Chartres

Fontainebleau

GERMANY

Rennes

Le Mans

Orleans

Vosges Mts

Mulhouse

Angers

R. Loire

Bourgogne
(Burgundy)

Dijon

R. Saone

Besancon

SWITZERLAND

Nantes

Tours

FRANCE

Jura Mts

Limoges

Clermont-Ferrand

Lyon

▲ Mt Blanc
4807m

OF BISCAY

▲ Mt Dore
1886m

Saint-Etienne

Perigueux

Grenoble

ITALY

Massif Central

Bordeaux

R. Dordogne

Cevennes Mts

R. Rhone

French Alps

MONACO

R. Garonne

Nimes

Avignon

Nice

Bayonne
Biarritz

Toulouse

Montpelier

Arles

Cannes

Lourdes

Carcassonne

Toulon

Pyrenees

Narbonne

Marseille

ANDORRA

Perpignan

▲ 2710m

SPAIN

MEDITERRANEAN SEA

CORSICA
(France)

0   200 kms

0   100 miles

15

Spain and Portugal

Andorra

Portugal

Spain

Spain and Portugal make up the Iberian Peninsular. Spain's interior is a vast plateau, which means an area of high flat ground. It is crossed by several mountain ranges. But the highest peaks are in the Pyrenees in the north and the Sierra Nevada in the south. Fertile plains and sandy beaches surround the central plateau. Spain is divided into several regions. One of these is Andalusia in the south. It is famous for its lively fiestas and flamenco dancers.

Spain's warm climate and golden sands attract thousands of tourists to its coastal resorts. Many Spaniards work in the tourist industry, but most work on the land. Some farmers do everything by hand or with the help of a donkey or mule. The soil is very dry and needs to be constantly watered, or irrigated. Farmers grow wheat, rice, olives, potatoes, grapes and oranges.

Portugal borders Spain on the west. Most people are fishermen and farmers. Others work in the tourist industry or in factories where they process food and make textiles. There are large cork forests in Portugal and many vineyards. Cork and port, a special type of wine, are exported to countries all over the world.

LEFT: *The ruins of a 13th-century convent lie in the countryside of the Castellon region of eastern Spain.*

BAY OF BISCAY

FRANCE

Gijon

Coruna

Santander

San Sebastian

Oviedo

Bilbao

Andorra la Vella

2648m

Pamplona

ANDORRA

Santiago de Compostella

Pyrenees

3404m

Burgos

R. Ebro

Vigo

Zaragoza

Braga

Tarragona

Barcelona

R. Duero

orto

Valladolid

R. Douro

Salamanca

Segovia

2430m

Coimbra

1991m

2592m

Madrid

2019m

PORTUGAL

R. Tagus

Toledo

SPAIN

Valencia

R. Guadiana

MAJORCA

Palma

IBIZA

BALEARIC
ISLANDS

Setubal

Alicante

R. Segura

Murcia

MEDITERRANEAN SEA

Córdoba

R. Guadalquivir

Seville

Andalucia
(Andalusia)

Granada

Mt Mulhacen
3478m

Huelva

Sierra Nevada

Almeria

os

Albufeira

Malaga

Faro

Cadiz

Marbella

ATLANTIC OCEAN

GIBRALTAR
(Britain)

ALGERIA

0   80 kms

0   50 miles

MOROCCO

RIGHT: *Lisbon is the captial of Portugal
and the country's chief port. It is
situated on the estuary of the River
Tagus. The river flows right across
Portugal, starting in Spain.*

17

Germany, Switzerland and Austria

ABOVE: *A village in the Austrian Tyrol. The scenery is typical of the Alps, Europe's greatest mountain range.*

Austria

Germany

Liechtenstein

Switzerland

The Alps, the mountains that cross Switzerland and Austria, are famous for their spectacular scenery and sports like mountain climbing and skiing. Yet the landscape is not just made up of mountains. A great many wide, flat-bottomed valleys criss-cross the area. Even when there is snow on the mountain tops, fruit and vegetables can be grown quite easily because the valleys are sheltered and warm, especially on their south facing slopes. Dairy farming is also important in these valleys.

In Switzerland rivers are dammed to catch water, which is used to drive generators to make electricity for homes and factories. This type of power is called hydroelectricity. It is Switzerland's major natural resource.

After 1945, Germany was divided into two separate countries by a 900-kilometre wall that snaked south from Lubeck. In 1989, this wall was taken down and the country re-united in 1990. But the area once known as East Germany is much poorer than the western part. Most of Germany's richest areas lie in the west, close to the River Rhine and its tributaries. Here are many factories, where cars, machinery, electrical goods and chemicals are manufactured.

Most people north of the Alps speak German, though French, Italian and Romansch (a kind of Latin) are also spoken in parts of Switzerland.

RIGHT: *The manufacture of motor cars is one of Germany's most important industries. Here, a worker is employed on the assembly line at a car factory.*

BALTIC SEA

RTH SEA

Kiel •

• Rostock

Lubeck •

• Bremerhaven   • Schwerin

◉Hamburg

• Oldenburg

R. Elbe

• Bremen

R. Oder

POLAND

R. Ems

R. Weser

R. Aller

Hanover •

R. Spree

◻Berlin

NETHERLANDS

• Brunswick

R. Oder

• Munster • Bielefeld

Harz Mts

• Magdeburg

Dortmund •

Duisburg •

• Bochum   Kassel •

• Dessau

Krefeld • • Essen

• Halle   Cottbus •

n-gladbach •

Dusseldorf • • Wuppertal

Leipzig • • Gera

• Siegen

• Erfurt   R. Elbe   Dresden

UM

• Cologne

• Dresden

Aachen • • Bonn

R. Rhine

Karl-Marx-Stadt •

• Koblenz

GERMANY

Wiesbaden • Frankfurt •

LUXEMBOURG

• Mainz • Offenbach   R. Main

R. Mosel

• Darmstadt • Würzburg

Saarbrucken •

• Mannheim   • Nuremberg

CZECHOSLOVAKIA

R. Rhine

• Karlsruhe

Regensburg •

Black Forest

• Stuttgart   R. Danube

FRANCE

Augsburg •

R. Danube

• Freiburg

◉Munich   Linz • Vienna ◻

Bodensee

(L. Constance)

Basel •   LIECHTENSTEIN

• Salzburg   AUSTRIA

Jura Mts • Zurich

R. Rhine

HUNGARY

Lucerne • ◻Vaduz   • Innsbruck   The Alps

Berne • 4274m▲

Lausanne   SWITZERLAND   The Alps

Gross Glockner   • Graz

Lake Leman   Gross Glockner

(L. Geneva) R. Rhone   ▲4094m   3797m

▲4634m

Matterhorn   ITALY

4478m

0   200 kms

0   100 miles

YUGOSLAVIA

19

Central and Eastern Europe

Czechoslo-vakia

Hungary

Poland

Poland and Hungary are countries with vast areas of flat land. The fertile lowlands are good for farming and herds of cattle and horses graze on the wide open plains. Between these two countries lies Czechoslovakia. Here the snow-capped Carpathian Mountains tower over the land.

Poland is the largest country in this region. It is a major world producer of coal. There are many big ports on the Baltic Sea where ships are built. Czechoslovakia and Hungary do not have any seaside but the River Danube links them with the sea. Barges carry goods along it to other countries in Europe.

ABOVE: *A winter view of Budapest, Hungary's capital city. It is made up of the old cities of Buda and Pest, which are divided by the River Danube.*

In the countries of central and eastern Europe, potatoes, wheat and sugar-beet are important crops on the farms. But, since World War II, more and more Poles, Czechs and Hungarians have been leaving their farmlands to work in mines and factories.

After 1945 Czechoslovakia, Poland and Hungary became communist countries. In communist countries, the government runs most factories and mines, and many farms. In the late 1980s many people in central and eastern Europe became dissatisfied with the communist system and the communist governments of these countries were overthrown in 1989.

RIGHT: *The rolling hills of southern Poland are scattered with many small farms. The fertile land supports a variety of crops, especially potatoes, rye, barley and wheat.*

SWEDEN

BALTIC SEA

LITHUANIA

Gdansk
Koszalin

Szczecin

R. Netze • Bydgoszcz

Bialystok

R. Vistula

R. Bug

• Poznan

☒ Warsaw

POLAND

• Lodz

GERMANY

R. Neisse

R. Oder

Wroclaw

• Lublin

Katowice

Krakow

Prague ☒

R. Elbe

▲ 1492m

• Ostrava

R. Vltava

Pizen

CZECHOSLOVAKIA

• Brno

R. Van

Carpathian Mts

▲ 2655m

former
USSR

• Kosice

Bratislava • R. Danube

Miskolc

• Nyiregyhaza

AUSTRIA

Gyor

☒ Budapest

Debrecen

ITALY

Lake
Balaton

HUNGARY

R. Danube

R. Tisza

ROMANIA

YUGOSLAVIA

Pecs

Szeged

| 0 | | 200 kms |
| 0 | | 100 miles |

The Balkans and Romania

Albania

Bulgaria

Bulgaria, Yugoslavia, Albania and Greece make up the Balkan countries. Romania borders Bulgaria and Yugoslavia. Yugoslavia was formed in 1918 from six republics: Bosnia and Herzegovenia, Croatia, Macedonia, Montenegro, Serbia and Croatia. Most of the people are Slavs and many different languages are spoken. A war between the Serbs and the Croats began in 1991, and the republics of Croatia and Slovenia declared their independence later that year. The republics of Bosnia and Herzegovenia, and Macedonia followed in 1992.

Greece consists of the mainland and over 1400 islands, including Crete. It is very mountainous and sheep and goats graze over the hills. Only one-third of Greece is suitable for farming. But in spite of this nearly half of the people live on the land. Many farmers grow grapes for making wine. Sometimes the grapes are picked, left to dry in the hot sun, then sold as raisins, currants or sultanas.

Bulgaria, Yugoslavia, Albania and Romania are also very mountainous. But, unlike Greece, the mountains are covered with forests where wolves, wild boars and bears still live. Beneath the valuable forests there are rich deposits of copper, zinc, coal and oil. Many people work in industry turning these minerals into useful products. Many others, especially in Albania, work on farms in the valleys, growing wheat, sugar beet, maize and potatoes.

Yugoslavia and Greece have beautiful beaches and islands, which attract thousands of holiday-makers. Greece also has fascinating ruins from the times of the Ancient Greeks, over two thousand years ago.

Greece

Romania

Yugoslavia

ABOVE: *The village of Sveti Stefan was built on a promontory in the Adriatic Sea. The beautiful beach is typical of Yugoslavia's coastline.*

RIGHT: *This coastal land on the Greek island of Andros has been terraced for farming. The island lies in the Aegean Sea.*

0 __ 200 kms
0 __ 100 miles

former
USSR

HUNGARY

• Cluj

Carpathian Mts

• Iasi

R. Drava
riglav ▲SLOVENIA
363m   • Ljubljana
          • Zagreb
• Rijeka CROATIA R. Sava

R. Tisa

• Timisoara

Transylvania Alps • Brasov

▲ 2518m

• Galati
• Ploesti

• Belgrade

ROMANIA

BOSNIA/
HERZEGOVINA

• Craiova

⊡Bucharest
• Constanta

• Sarajevo

R. Danube • Ruse

Split

Dinaric Alps YUGOSLAVIA

R. Morava

• Nis

ADRIATIC
SEA

▲ 2522m

SERBIA

R. Iskar

BULGARIA • Varna

Sofia ⊡

Balkan Mts

Dubrovnik

2692m

2496m

MONTENEGRO   ▲   ▲
                    MACEDONIA

Mt Musala
2925m ▲

Plovdiv
R. Maritsa

• Burgas

• Skopje

Rhodope Mts

R. Vardar

Durres •
Tirana •

ALBANIA
2480m
2637m▲

• Thessaloniki

Mt Olympus
▲
2917m

• Lárisa

CORFU

Pindus Mts

GREECE

TURKEY

LESVOS

AEGEAN
SEA

Delphi •

• Patras

2376m▲

Piraeus • Athens

Olympia •

Corinth

MYKONOS

IONIAN SEA

• Sparta

NAXOS

Kalamata •

RHODES

Iraklion
CRETE

MEDITERRANEAN SEA

Note: at the time of printing the situation in
the former Yugoslav republics was uncertain.
The borders of the Federal Republic of
Yugoslavia are still being disputed.

23

Italy and its Neighbours

Italy

Malta

Italy is shaped like a boot kicking a ball. Sicily is the 'ball'. Sicily, Sardinia and many smaller islands are also part of Italy. The Apennine Mountains run down the back of Italy like a spine. There are several volcanic mountains in Italy. The best known is Mount Vesuvius, near the city of Naples in southern Italy.

Tourists flock to Italy to enjoy the warm climate, to see the beautiful buildings and paintings, and to visit the ruins of Ancient Rome. In the north there are large industrial cities, such as Milan and Turin. Italians make textiles and cars to sell to other countries. In the south farmers grow olives, citrus fruit, and grapes for making wine.

Vatican City is the smallest country in Europe. It is the home of the Pope, the head of the Roman Catholic Church. San Marino is another tiny country in Italy and Malta is an island country in the Mediterranean Sea.

ABOVE: *The church of Santa Maria della Salute stands beside the Grand Canal in Venice. The city has more than 100 canals. Boats called gondolas transport people around the city.*

San Marino

Vatican City

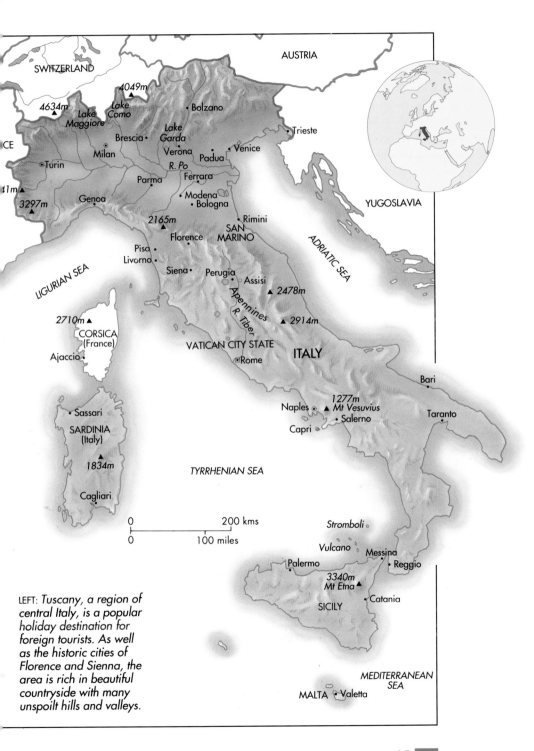

SWITZERLAND

AUSTRIA

4049m

4634m

Lake Como

Bolzano

Lake Maggiore

Lake Garda

Trieste

Brescia

Verona

Padua

Venice

ICE

Milan

Turin

R. Po

Ferrara

YUGOSLAVIA

11m

Parma

Modena

3297m

Genoa

Bologna

Rimini

2165m

SAN MARINO

Florence

ADRIATIC SEA

Pisa

LIGURIAN SEA

Livorno

Siena

Perugia

Assisi

2478m

Apennines

R. Tiber

2914m

2710m

CORSICA
(France)

VATICAN CITY STATE

ITALY

Ajaccio

Rome

Bari

1277m
Mt Vesuvius

Naples

Sassari

Salerno

Taranto

SARDINIA
(Italy)

Capri

1834m

TYRRHENIAN SEA

Cagliari

0   200 kms

0   100 miles

Stromboli

Vulcano

Messina

Palermo

Reggio

3340m
Mt Etna

Catania

SICILY

MEDITERRANEAN SEA

MALTA   Valetta

LEFT: *Tuscany, a region of central Italy, is a popular holiday destination for foreign tourists. As well as the historic cities of Florence and Sienna, the area is rich in beautiful countryside with many unspoilt hills and valleys.*

25

Russia and its Neighbours

Estonia

Latvia

Lithuania

Former USSR

Russia is the largest country in the world. Until 1992 it formed the biggest state of the Union of Soviet Socialist Republics, the USSR. The USSR was more the twice the size of Canada, the world's second largest country, and covered one-sixth of the world's total land surface.

In 1991 the Baltic states of Latvia, Estonia and Lithuania broke away from the USSR and became independent countries. The Commonwealth of Independent States was then set up by Russia, The Ukraine and Byelorussia. Russia and the other 14 states that formed the USSR are made up of people of over 100 groups – Ukranians, Uzbeks, Kazakhs and many others. Over 60 languages are used, but Russian is spoken in most places.

After the communist revolution in 1917, the USSR developed from an old-fashioned farming country into a powerful industrial nation. Large resources of coal, oil and natural gas provide fuel for the huge numbers of factories and industrial plants. There are also many mineral deposits in the Ural mountains, The Ukraine, Georgia and Kazakhstan.

One-quarter of Russia and the neighbouring states is farmland. Farmers work either on enormous state-owned farms or on smaller collectives producing huge quantities of wheat, rye, barley, meat and dairy products.

0   1000 kms
0   600 miles   AR

NORWEGIAN SEA

NORWAY
SWEDEN
FINLAND
ESTONIA • Tallinn   ⊙ St Petersh
LATVIA • Riga
LITHUANIA • Vilnius   Moscow
POLAND • Minsk   ⊡
BYELORUSSIA
Kiev ⊙   R. Don
UKRAINE
Kishinev   ⊙ Kharkov
• Odessa   Donetsk Vol
MOLDOVA   Astrakhan
Sevastopol •   Caucasus C
BLACK SEA
Mt Elbrus, 5633m   Tbilisi •
GEORGIA   Yereva
ARMENIA
TURKEY

LEFT: *The Pamir mountain range makes up 90 per cent of Tadzhikistan, a republic of the former USSR. It includes Communism Peak, the highest mountain in the former USSR.*

RANZ JOSEF LAND

SEVERNAYA
ZEMLYA

NEW SIBERIAN
ISLES

EAST SIBERIAN
SEA

NOVAYA
ZEMLYA

KARA
SEA

LAPTEV
SEA

R. Kolyma

elsk

R. Lena

SIBERIA

RUSSIA

Ural Mountains

R. Ob

R. Yenisey

SEA OF
OKHOTSK

Sverdlovsk

Tomsk

Chelyabinsk

Omsk

yshev

Novosibirsk

Lake
Baikal

R. Amur

Irkutsk

Khabarovsk

AZERBAIJAN

KAZAKHSTAN

Lake
Balkhash

CHINA

ARAL
SEA

UZBEKISTAN

MONGOLIA

Vladivostok

Frunze

Alma Ata

Tien Shan Mts

SEA OF
JAPAN

Tashkent

KHIRGHIZIA

Bukhara

Samarkand

Pamir Mts

TADZHIKISTAN

JAPAN

Kum Mts

AFGHANISTAN

TURKMENISTAN

RIGHT: *The colourful
minarets are part of St
Basil's Cathedral, which is
situated near Red Square
in Moscow, the Russian
capital. The building is
now a museum.*

Southwest Asia

Bahrain

Cyprus

Iran

Iraq

Israel

Jordan

Kuwait

Lebanon

Oman

RIGHT: *Until 1990 Yemen was divided into two separate countries. This cemetery in Hadramaut is in the eastern part of the country in what used to be South Yemen.*

Most people living in the Middle East are Arab. Their language is Arabic and their religion is Islam. Even in the non-Arab countries, Iran and Turkey, the people are Muslim. Many Christians live in Cyprus and Lebanon and most of the people in Israel are Jewish. The different religions of the people living in this area has been the cause of constant trouble between them for many years.

On the map you can see that most of this area is desert. Many of the people are farmers and the lack of rainfall is a serious problem. On the Mediterranean coast, in river valleys and around oases, farms are irrigated with water from rivers and wells. But it is oil and not farming which has brought wealth to many countries in this area. Saudi Arabia alone has a quarter of the world's oil reserves.

Many pilgrims visit the Middle East. Jerusalem, the capital of Israel, is a holy city to Jews, Christians and Muslims. Mecca and Medina in Saudi Arabia are Muslim holy cities.

LEFT: *Exporting oil has made Saudi Arabia rich. Oil refineries treat crude oil pumped through long pipelines from wells inland or extracted from the Persian Gulf.*

RIGHT: *Most of the land in Kuwait is desert. Towers are used to store water, which is in short supply.*

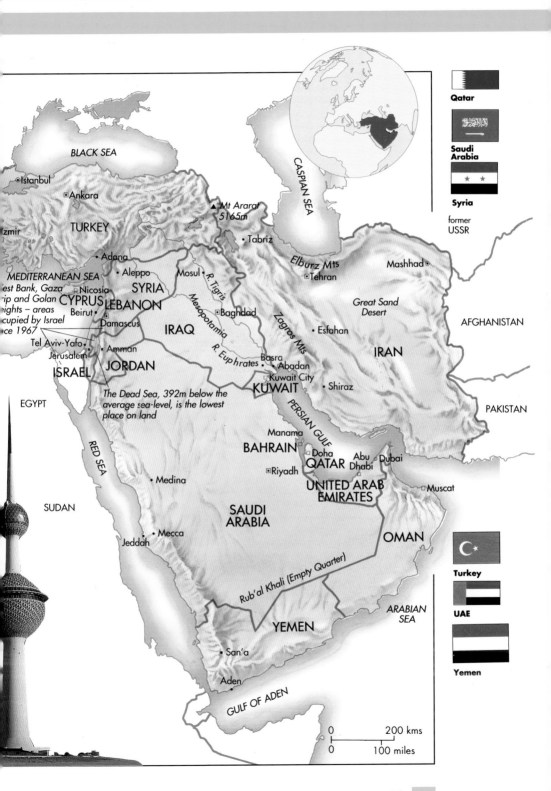

BLACK SEA

•Istanbul

□Ankara

Izmir

TURKEY

▲ Mt Ararat
5165m

• Tabriz

CASPIAN SEA

• Adana

Elburz Mts

Mashhad ⊙

MEDITERRANEAN SEA

est Bank, Gaza
rip and Golan
eights – areas
cupied by Israel
ce 1967

Nicosia

CYPRUS

• Aleppo

SYRIA

LEBANON

Beirut □

Damascus

Mosul •

R. Tigris

⊡Tehran

Great Sand
Desert

□Baghdad

Mesopotamia

IRAQ

AFGHANISTAN

Tel Aviv-Yafo •

Jerusalem •

ISRAEL

JORDAN

• Amman

R. Euphrates

Zagros Mts

• Esfahan

IRAN

Basra
• Abadan

□Kuwait City

KUWAIT

• Shiraz

PAKISTAN

The Dead Sea, 392m below the
average sea-level, is the lowest
place on land

EGYPT

PERSIAN GULF

RED SEA

Manama

BAHRAIN

□Riyadh

Doha

QATAR

Abu
Dhabi

• Dubai

UNITED ARAB
EMIRATES

• Muscat

SUDAN

• Medina

SAUDI
ARABIA

OMAN

• Mecca

Jeddah

Rub'al Khali (Empty Quarter)

ARABIAN
SEA

YEMEN

• San'a

Aden

GULF OF ADEN

0   200 kms

0   100 miles

Qatar

Saudi
Arabia

Syria

former
USSR

Turkey

UAE

Yemen

India and its Neighbours

Afghanistan

Bangladesh

Bhutan

India

Maldives

Nepal

Pakistan

Sri Lanka

LEFT: *The Taj Mahal in Agra, northern India, is said to be one of the world's most beautiful buildings. It is made out of white marble and is the tomb of the wife of an Indian ruler.*

This region contains the highest mountain range in the world – the Himalayas. It forms the boundary with Tibet and China and contains Mount Everest, the world's highest peak. On the map opposite you can trace the paths of three great rivers. They begin in the Himalayas and are the Ganges, the Indus and the Brahmaputra.

India, Pakistan and Bangladesh are thickly populated nations. Farming is the main occupation, but there is never enough food for the huge numbers of people. Many children start to work in the fields with their parents when they are very young. Farming methods are often very simple because there is little money for machinery or fertilizers. The monsoon climate is also a problem. It means that twice every year there are huge downpours of rain. If the rain is too heavy, it washes away crops. If the rains come too late, the crops may die. The Indian, Pakistani and Bangladeshi governments are trying to set up more factories to counteract the effects of the rains.

Religion is important in the everyday life of the people in this region. Most Indians and Nepalese are Hindu while most Pakistanis and Afghans and many Bangladeshis are Muslim, followers of Islam.

ABOVE: *A woman picks tea in Sri Lanka. Rice, cocnuts and rubber are the other main agricultural products.*

0 ____ 1000 kms
0 ____ 600 miles

former USSR

Hindu Kush

K2 8611m

Herat

Kabul • Khyber Pass

Srinagar •

Karakoram Range

AFGHANISTAN

Islamabad •
Rawalpindi •

Kandahar •

CHINA

Mt Everest, 8863m, is the highest mountain in the world

TIBET

Nanda Devi 7817m

Amritsar
Lahore •

Faisalabad ◉

R. Helmand

R. Indus

R. Sutlej

PAKISTAN

Meerut •

New Delhi ☐ Delhi

Jaipur •

Thar Desert

Jodhpur •

Agra •

Himalayas

Lucknow •
Kanpur •

NEPAL

Mt Kanchenjunga 8597m

Thimbu •

BHUTAN

Katmandu •

R. Brahmaputra

Hyderabad ◉

Karachi ◉

Allahabad •

R. Ganges

Benares •

Patna •

BANGLADESH

RABIAN SEA

Ahamadabad •

Indore •

Bhopal •

Calcutta ◉

Dhaka ☐

Chittagong •

MYANMAR (BURMA)

ELOW: *The Khumbu lacier near Mount verest in the imalayas.*

R. Narmada

Surat •

Nagpur •

R. Mahanadi

Cuttack •

INDIA

Bombay ◉

Poona ◉

R. Godavari

BAY OF BENGAL

R. Krishna

Hyderabad •

Deccan Plateau

Eastern Ghats

Goa •

Western Ghats

Bangalore ◉

Madras •

Mysore •

Calicut •

Cochin •

Madurai •

Trivandrum •

INDIAN OCEAN

Colombo •

SRI LANKA

China and its Neighbours

Nearly a quarter of all the people in the world live in China. It has more people than any other nation. Most people live in the fertile valleys of the Huang He and Chang Jiang (Yangtze) rivers and along the crowded coast. China is the third largest country in the world. It stretches from the plateau of Central Asia to the Pacific Ocean.

Since 1949, China has had a communist government. Mao Zedong (Mao Tse-tung) was the leader of the government until his death in 1976. By encouraging everyone to put the needs of the community first, he helped turn China from a poor agricultural country into a great industrial one. Factories have been built all over China and many of the workers make iron and steel. But farming is still important and two-thirds of the population are farmers.

Mongolia lies to the north of China. Most of the country is desert and the few people living there are wandering herdsmen. Many of them live in large round tents made from animal skins. On the map you can also see the peninsula of Korea. It is divided into two countries – North Korea and South Korea. South Korea is rapidly developing as an industrial nation.

ABOVE: *Many of Hong Kong's people make their living through trade.*

China

Mongolia

North Korea

South Korea

Taiwan

former USSR

Tien
Tarim

Ku

TI

Himalaya Mts

NEPAL

INDIA

0 ____ 400 kms
0 ____ 200 miles

Altai Mts

rumqi

MONGOLIA

• Ulan Bator

Gobi Desert

Tarim Basin

INNER MONGOLIA

• Hohhot

MANCHURIA

• Qiqihar

◉ Harbin

R. Liao

• Jilin

Shenyang ◉ Fushun
• Anshan

NORTH
KOREA

• Pyongyang

Great Wall of China

• Baotou

Beijing ◻
(Peking)

Tangshan

Tianjin

Dalian
(Luda)

◻ Seoul

SOUTH
KOREA

◉ Pusan

n Tagh Mts

Taiyuan

Jinan •

• Qingdao

YELLOW
SEA

n Mts

• Lanzhou

Huang He (Yellow River)

Xi'an •

Luyang

Zhengzhou

• Xuzhou

CHINA

R. Lanchang Jiang (Mekong)

R. Nu Jiang (Salween)

Chengdu ◉

R. Chang Jiang (Yangtze)

Nanjing ◉

• Shanghai

Lhasa

maputra

• Yichang

◉ Wuhan

• Chongqing

Hangzhou •

EAST CHINA SEA

TAN

• Nanchang

• Changsha

MYANMAR
(Burma)

• Guiyang

• Fuzhou

◻ Taipei

• Kunming

R. Xi-Jiang

Guangzhou
◉ (Canton)

TAIWAN

◉ Kaohsiung

VIETNAM

• Nanning

MACAO
(Portugal)

HONG KONG (U.K.)

PACIFIC OCEAN

LAOS

• Hanoi

SOUTH CHINA SEA

HAINAN

LEFT: *This spectacular limestone
landscape shows part of the
Li River valley about 400
kilometres southeast of the city
of Guiyang in southern China.*

Japan

Japan consists of four main islands and about 3000 smaller ones. From one end of the main islands to the other, there runs a volcanic mountain chain. Many of the volcanoes are still active. Mount Fuji, the highest peak, is a volcano, but it has not erupted since 1707. Earthquakes are common in Japan. There are over 1000 each year, but most of them are only small tremors.

There is not much land suitable for farming in Japan, because it is so mountainous. Rice is the main food crop on the little land which is cultivated. Fishing is important for it provides food for the large population. Japanese cooks use shark fins and eels to make soup and seaweed is also a favourite dish.

Japan is the wealthiest country in Asia because it has such an efficient manufacturing industry. Japanese workers make more cameras, televisions and ships than any other country. Most of the people live on the coastal plains, where there are many crowded industrial cities. But Japan also has many peaceful temples and beautiful gardens.

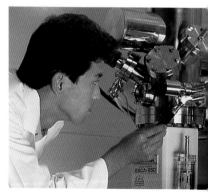

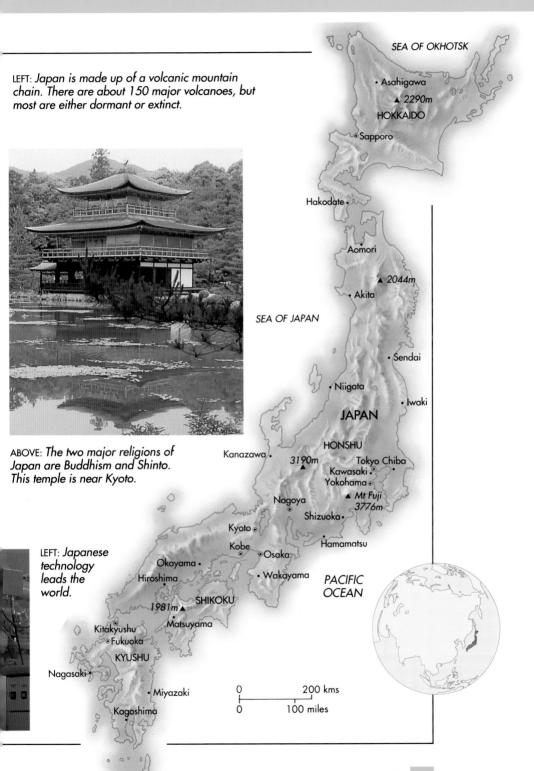

LEFT: *Japan is made up of a volcanic mountain chain. There are about 150 major volcanoes, but most are either dormant or extinct.*

ABOVE: *The two major religions of Japan are Buddhism and Shinto. This temple is near Kyoto.*

LEFT: *Japanese technology leads the world.*

SEA OF OKHOTSK

· Asahigawa

▲ 2290m

HOKKAIDO

⊙ Sapporo

Hakodate ·

Aomori

▲ 2044m

· Akita

SEA OF JAPAN

· Sendai

· Niigata

· Iwaki

JAPAN

HONSHU

Kanazawa ·

3190m ▲

Tokyo Chiba
Kawasaki ⊡ ·
Yokohama ⊙

Nagoya
⊙

▲ Mt Fuji
3776m

Shizuoka ·

Kyoto ⊙

Kobe
⊙   ⊙ Osaka

Hamamatsu

Okayama ·

· Wakayama

PACIFIC
OCEAN

Hiroshima
·

1981m ▲
SHIKOKU

Matsuyama

Kitakyushu ⊙
⊙ Fukuoka

KYUSHU

Nagasaki ·

· Miyazaki

Kagoshima ·

| 0 | | 200 kms |
| 0 | 100 miles | |

Southeast Asia

Brunei

Cambodia

Indonesia

Laos

Malaysia

Much of Southeast Asia is made up of volcanic islands. Indonesia has over 3000 islands and the Philippines more than 7000. All the countries have a similar hot, wet climate and much of the land is mountainous.

Southeast Asia is a heavily populated region. Many people live in stilt houses in fertile river valleys. Peasant farmers cut terraces into the hillsides where they grow rice, the main food crop. The slopes which are not tilled are covered in forest. There are also large rubber, coffee and tobacco plantations in Indonesia, Malaysia and Myanmar (Burma).

Mining is another important occupation in this region. Malaysia produces one-third of the world's supply of tin. It is one of the richest countries in Southeast Asia. The standard of living is also very high in Singapore. This small island nation has one of the world's busiest ports, and is an important centre for oil-refining. But many people in Vietnam and its neighbouring countries are very poor because they suffered years of war.

Music, dance, drama and hand-made crafts keep alive the ancient stories and legends of Southeast Asia. Islam and Buddhism are the main religions in this area.

Myanmar (Burma)

Philippines

Singapore

ABOVE: *Latex oozes out of the bark of a rubber tree. Forests in Southeast Asia produce most of the world's natural rubber.*

RIGHT: *Wooden houses are built on stilts in some parts of the Philippines. The owners are fishermen.*

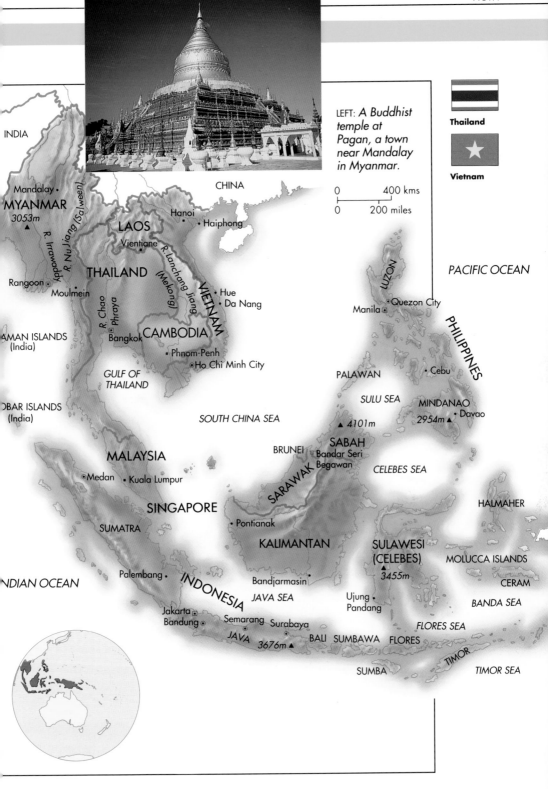

LEFT: *A Buddhist temple at Pagan, a town near Mandalay in Myanmar.*

Thailand

Vietnam

INDIA

Mandalay •
MYANMAR
▲ 3053m

R. Irrawaddy

R. Nu Jiang (Salween)

CHINA

LAOS

Hanoi •
• Haiphong

Vientiane •

R. Lanchang Jiang
(Mekong)

THAILAND

VIETNAM

Rangoon •
• Moulmein

R. Chao
Phraya

• Hue
• Da Nang

Bangkok ◻

CAMBODIA

MAN ISLANDS
(India)

• Phnom-Penh
• Ho Chi Minh City

**GULF OF
THAILAND**

0   400 kms
0   200 miles

PACIFIC OCEAN

LUZON

•Quezon City
Manila ◻

PHILIPPINES

PALAWAN

• Cebu

SOUTH CHINA SEA

SULU SEA

MINDANAO
2954m ▲ • Davao

▲ 4101m

OBAR ISLANDS
(India)

MALAYSIA

BRUNEI •
SABAH
Bandar Seri
Begawan

CELEBES SEA

•Medan • Kuala Lumpur

SARAWAK

HALMAHER

SINGAPORE

• Pontianak

SUMATRA

KALIMANTAN

**SULAWESI
(CELEBES)**
▲ 3455m

MOLUCCA ISLANDS

CERAM

NDIAN OCEAN

Palembang •

INDONESIA

Bandjarmasin •

JAVA SEA

Ujung •
Pandang

BANDA SEA

Jakarta ◻
Bandung ◉

Semarang
JAVA Surabaya
3676m ▲

FLORES SEA

BALI SUMBAWA FLORES

SUMBA

TIMOR

TIMOR SEA

Canada

Canada is the second largest country in the world: only Russia is larger. Vast areas in the far north are uninhabited and only a small number of trappers and fishermen live in the snow-blanketed forests around the Hudson Bay. Most Canadians live in the south, not far from the USA border, where the climate is warmer. The Prairie Provinces of Alberta, Saskatchewan and Manitoba lie west of the Great Lakes. They are sometimes called the 'bread basket of the world' because wheat farms stretch as far as the eye can see.

Canada's original people arrived there over 20,000 years ago. They came from Asia and their descendants today are the North American Indians and the Inuit (Eskimos). British and French settlers did not arrive until the 17th century, but today 97 per cent of the population is of European descent.

Large deposits of minerals, such as asbestos, zinc, silver and nickel, as well as fertile plains and rich forests help make Canada one of the wealthiest countries in the world. Canadians are proud too, of their beautiful lakes and mountains and the cool, clean air of their forests.

ABOVE:
Vancouver is a port on the Pacific Ocean. It is the third largest city in Canada.

ALASKA (USA)

YUKON TERRITORY

Dawson

Whitehorse

Mt Logan 6050m

Mackenzie Mountains

Yukon R.

BRITISH COLUMBIA

Rocky Mountains

Prince Geo

PACIFIC OCEAN

VANCOUVER I.

Victoria ★ • Vancouver

QUEEN ELIZABETH ISLANDS

MELVILLE I.

BANKS I.

DEVON I.

BAFFIN BAY

VICTORIA ISLAND I.

BAFFIN ISLAND

Lake

NORTHWEST TERRITORIES

ATLANTIC OCEAN

Yellowknife

Slave Lake

HUDSON STRAIT

ake Athabasca

Churchill R.

HUDSON BAY

Churchill

LABRADOR

NADA

Nelson R.

St John's

SKATCHEWAN

MANITOBA

NEWFOUNDLAND

onton

Saskatchewan R.

QUEBEC

St Lawrence R.

PRINCE
EDWARD I.

Saskatoon

Lake
Winnipeg

ONTARIO

NEW
BRUNSWICK

Charlottetown

Regina

Quebec

NOVA SCOTIA

Winnipeg

Thunder Bay

Fredericton

Lake Superior

Montreal

Halifax

Sault Ste Marie

Ottawa

Sudbury

Lake
Huron

Toronto

Lake Michigan

Hamilton

Lake Ontario
Niagara Falls

Lake Erie

```
0                    800 kms
|_____|
0                    500 miles     • = provincial capital
```

LEFT: *Red Rock Canyon forms part
of the Rocky Mountains in the
Canadian province of Alberta. The
Rockies stretch from Alaska through
western Canada and the USA. They
contain rich mineral deposits.*

39

USA

The United States of America is the fourth largest country in the world and has the fourth largest population and land area. It is divided into 50 states and includes Alaska in the northwest and Hawaii, a group of islands in the Pacific Ocean.

Like Canada, the USA was first settled by Indians whose ancestors came from Asia. In the 18th and 19th centuries, large numbers of settlers came to the 'New World' from Europe in search of a better way of life. These people first settled on the east coast and started the first 13 states. Black Africans were brought over to the USA to work on cotton and tobacco plantations in the south.

ABOVE: *Skyscrapers dominate the Manhattan skyline of New York City. Manhattan's landmarks include the World Trade Centre and the Empire State Building.*

RIGHT: *Cattle and sheep graze beneath the Rocky Mountains in Colorado. Beef cattle, the most important farming product in the USA, are raised on huge ranches in the western states.*

CANADA

MONTANA

Missouri R.

Billings

Grand Teton
4196m

WYOMING

Mountains

Casper

Cheyenne

Denver

S. Platte R.

Pikes
Peak 4301m

Pueblo

COLORADO

Colorado
Springs

Sante Fe

Albuquerque

NEW MEXICO

El Paso

NORTH
DAKOTA

Bismarck

SOUTH DAKOTA

Pierre

Rapid City

NEBRASKA

Omaha

Lincoln

Platte R.

Arkansas R.

KANSAS

Topeka

Wichita

Amarillo

Oklahoma
City

OKLAHOMA

Tulsa

Fort Smith

ARKANSAS

Little Rock

Red R.

Fort Worth • • Dallas

Abilene

TEXAS

Austin

Houston

San Antonio

Rio Grande

Corpus Christi

MEXICO

MINNESOTA

Lake Superior

Minneapolis

St. Paul

WISCONSIN

Mississippi R.

Madison

Milwaukee

IOWA

Davenport

Sioux
City

Des Moines

ILLINOIS

Springfield

Kansas City

St Louis

Evansville

Jefferson City

MISSOURI

Springfield

Mississippi R.

Memphis

MICHIGAN

Lake Huron

Lake Michigan

Grand
Rapids

Lansing

Detroit

Lake Erie

Toledo

Cleveland

OHIO

Columbus

INDIANA

Indianapolis

Cincinnati

Louisville

Frankfort

KENTUCKY

Nashville

TENNESSEE

Tennessee R.

Birmingham

ALABAMA

Montgomery

MISSISSIPPI

Jackson

LOUISIANA

Baton Rouge

New Orleans

Atlanta

GEORGIA

Columbus

Lake Ontario

Buffalo

NEW YORK

Pittsburgh

PENNSYLVANIA

Ohio R.

WEST
VIRGINIA

Baltimore

Charleston

VIRGINIA

Richmond

Appalachian

NORTH
CAROLINA

Charlotte

Raleigh

Columbia

SOUTH CAROLINA

Charleston

Savannah

Jacksonville

FLORIDA

Tallahassee

Orlando

Tampa

Fort Lauderdale

Miami

GULF OF MEXICO

MAINE

Augusta

Bangor

Montpelier

N.H.

Portland

Concord

Boston

Syracuse

Albany

MASS.

Providence

RHODE
ISLAND

Hartford

CONN.

Newark

Long Island

NEW
JERSEY

New York City

Trenton

Philadelphia

Dover

DELAWARE

Annapolis

MARYLAND

Washington D.C.

Norfolk

Mountains

ATLANTIC OCEAN

Kilometres

0   500

0   300

Miles

KAUAI

OAHU

Honolulu

MAUI

HAWAII

HAWAII

Mt McKinley 6194m

Anchorage

Juneau

ALASKA

41

USA

Gradually people with pioneering spirits ventured westwards and new states were formed. Some farmed on the mid-western plains while explorers and miners travelled through the Rocky Mountains all the way to the Pacific coast. Today people from countries all over the world live in the USA, although the majority of the population is descended from Europeans.

The United States has an extremely varied climate, from arctic conditions in Alaska, to the hot deserts of the southwest. The landscape features high mountain ranges, vast plains, and the five Great Lakes.

Like their Canadian neighbours, most Americans have a high standard of living. The USA is an extremely wealthy country. It has large resources of oil, gas, coal, and many metals, huge farms and plantations and more factories than any other country in the world.

The largest city in the USA is New York, which is on the east coast. Other important cities include Chicago in the north and Los Angeles on the west coast.

ABOVE: *Huge, steep, flat-topped hills loom over the dry earth of Monument Valley in the states of Arizona and Utah. They are made of red sandstone and were formed by the wind gradually wearing away the rock.*

LEFT: *Football is extremely popular in the USA. The players wear helmets and thick pads under their clothing to protect them from injury.*

STATES OF USA

State	Popular name	Capital
Alabama	Yellowhammer State	Montgomery
Alaska	Last Frontier	Juneau
Arizona	Grand Canyon State	Phoenix
Arkansas	Land of Opportunity	Little Rock
California	Golden State	Sacremento
Colorado	Centennial State	Denver
Connecticut	Constitution State	Hartford
Delaware	First State	Dover
Florida	Sunshine State	Tallahassee
Georgia	Empire State of the South	Atlanta
Hawaii	Aloha State	Honolulu
Idaho	Gem State	Boise
Illinois	Land of Lincoln	Springfield
Indiana	Hoosier State	Indianapolis
Iowa	Hawkeye State	Des Moines
Kansas	Sunflower State	Topeka
Kentucky	Bluegrass State	Frankfort
Louisiana	Pelican State	Baton Rouge
Maine	Pine Tree State	Augusta
Maryland	Old Line State	Annapolis
Massachusetts	Bay State	Boston
Michigan	Wolverine State	Lansing
Minnesota	Gopher State	St Paul
Mississippi	Magnolia State	Jackson
Missouri	Show Me State	Jefferson City
Montana	Treasure State	Helena
Nebraska	Cornhusker State	Lincoln
Nevada	Silver State	Carson City
New Hampshire	Granite State	Concord
New Jersey	Garden State	Trenton
New Mexico	Land of Enchantment	Santa Fe
New York	Empire State	Albany
North Carolina	Tar Heel State	Raleigh
North Dakota	Flickertail State	Bismarck
Ohio	Buckeye State	Columbus
Oklahoma	Sooner State	Oklahoma City
Oregon	Beaver State	Salem
Pennsylvania	Keystone State	Harrisburg
Rhode Island	Little Rhody	Providence
South Carolina	Palmetto State	Columbia
South Dakota	Sunshine State	Pierre
Tennessee	Volunteer State	Nashville
Texas	Lone Star State	Austin
Utah	Beehive State	Salt Lake City
Vermont	Green Mountain State	Montpelier
Virgina	Old Dominion	Richmond
Washington	Evergreen State	Olympia
West Virginia	Mountain State	Charleston
Wisconsin	Badger State	Madison
Wyoming	Equality State	Cheyenne

Mexico, the Caribbean and Central America

Tijuana • Mexicali

Baja (Lower) California

GULF OF CALIFORNIA

• Hermosillo

Chi

Sierra Madre Occ

• Culiacan

Guadalajara

Antigua & Barbuda

Bahamas

Barbados

Mexico and the seven small countries that make up Central America form the land link between the United States and South America.

The people living in Central America and the islands of the West Indies are descendants of the original people or of Europeans and Black Africans.

LEFT: *Guatemala has the highest Indian population in Central America. They are the descendants of the Mayan Indians, who lived in this region over 1000 years ago.*

Cuba

Dominica

Dominican Republic

Grenada

Haiti

Most of them speak Spanish, English, French or American Indian languages. In 1492, when Christopher Columbus reached the islands in the Caribbean Sea, he thought he had sailed around the world to India. He called the people living there 'Indians' and the islands were named the West Indies.

Central America and the thousands of West Indian islands are mostly hot and mountainous. The climate is ideal for growing fruit, coffee, cotton, tobacco and sugar cane. Cuba is the largest of the West Indian islands and it is the third largest producer of sugar in the world. Many of the islands are popular holiday places because of their sunny climate and easy-going atmosphere.

In Mexico most people work on small farms. The main crop is maize. A favourite meal is tortillas, a pancake made from maize flour. Gold and other metals are mined in Mexico, but the most important industry is oil.

400 kms
200 miles

Belize   **Costa Rica**   **El Salvador**   **Guatemala**

Honduras   **Mexico**   **Nicaragua**   **Panama**

USA

Jamaica

Puerto Rico

• Monterrey

GULF OF MEXICO

Oriental

Potosi

• Tampico

ATLANTIC OCEAN

Nassau

STRAITS OF FLORIDA

BAHAMAS

xico
ty   Popocatepetl
▲ 5452m
• Puebla   • Veracruz

• Mérida

Yucatan
Peninsula

Havana

Santa Clara

Cienfuegos

CUBA

Camaguey
• Holguin

• Santiago de Cuba

GREATER

DOMINICAN   San Juan   BARBUDA
REPUBLIC   PUERTO   ST KITTS
RICO   NEVIS   ANTIGUA

del Sur

Acapulco

GULF OF
HONDURAS

BELIZE

Port-au-Prince

JAMAICA   HAITI
Kingston

Santo
Domingo

LEEWARD
ISLANDS

GU.

ANTILLES

LESSER ANTILLES

DOMINICA

MA.
BAR.

PACIFIC
OCEAN

GUATEMALA

Guatemala City •   San
Salvador •

EL
SALVADOR

Managua •

HONDURAS

• Tegucigalpa

NICARAGUA

Lake
Nicaragua

CARIBBEAN SEA

ST LUCIA

WINDWARD
ISLANDS

ST VINCENT

GRENADA

TRINIDAD
&
TOBAGO

BELOW: *Dense
mangrove swamps
cover large areas of
coastline in the Caribbean.*

San José •

COSTA RICA

Panama
Canal

• Panama City

PANAMA

COLOMBIA

GU. GUADELOUPE (France)
MA. MARTINIQUE (France)
BAR. BARBADOS

**St Kitts-
Nevis**

St Lucia

**St Vincent
&
Grenadines**

**Trinidad
& Tobago**

45

The Andean Countries

The Andes mountains rise above much of Colombia, Ecuador, Peru and Bolivia. They form high tablelands or plateaus where the climate is cool even though the Equator passes through Ecuador and Colombia. Many rivers that feed the Amazon river begin in the Andes and travel eastwards through thick tropical forests.

Bananas and coffee are grown on large plantations where the climate is hot and tropical. As transport across the mountains gets better, more people are living in the Amazon lowlands. Here they farm and work in mines. But much of the land is covered by thick forest and cannot be farmed.

Over 800 years ago the Andes were populated by the Incas. Gold and silver in the mountains attracted the Spaniards who eventually destroyed the Inca civilization. Today minerals are still important, especially tin mined in Bolivia. Peru also produces oil for exporting to other countries. Spanish is the official language spoken in the Andean countries.

Bolivia

Colombia

Ecuador

Peru

ABOVE: *The ruins of the ancient Inca city of Machu Picchu lie high in the Andes mountains of Peru.*

RIGHT: *Fruit is displayed on a market stall in Ecuador. As in all the Andean countries, a large proportion of the population is made up of Indians. Many of them still speak the old Indian languages.*

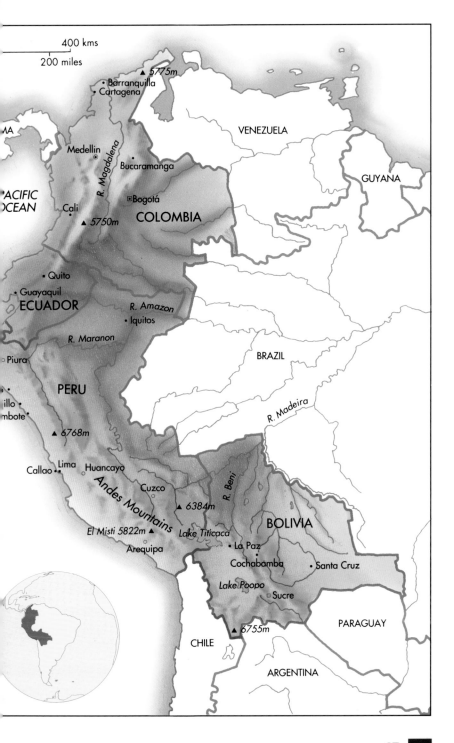

400 kms
200 miles

▲ 5775m
• Barranquilla
• Cartagena

VENEZUELA

GUYANA

PACIFIC
OCEAN

Medellin ◉
R. Magdalena
• Bucaramanga

Cali •
⊡ Bogotá
COLOMBIA
▲ 5750m

• Quito
• Guayaquil
ECUADOR

R. Amazon
• Iquitos

R. Maranon

Piura

BRAZIL

PERU

illo
mbote •

▲ 6768m

R. Madeira

Callao •
Lima
Huancayo

Andes Mountains
Cuzco

R. Beni

▲ 6384m

BOLIVIA

El Misti 5822m ▲
Lake Titicaca
• La Paz
Cochabamba •
• Santa Cruz

Arequipa

Lake Poopo
⊡ Sucre

PARAGUAY

▲ 6755m

CHILE

ARGENTINA

Brazil and its Neighbours

Brazil

**French
Guiana**

Guyana

Surinam

Venezuela

People of many different races live together in eastern South America. There are American Indians and mestizos, who are mixed Indian and European people. Other people are direct descendants of Europeans or Africans. Most of the early settlers were Spanish or Portuguese and most South Americans today speak one of these languages. Many people are also Roman Catholic.

Brazil is the largest country in South America. Much of the land is covered in thick Amazon rain forest. Most people live in big cities, such as Rio de Janeiro and São Paulo near the Atlantic coast. The northeastern part of Brazil is poorer. Land is owned by a few rich landlords who employ farmers. In bad years the farmers have to go to the cities in search of other work.

ABOVE: *High-rise buildings dominate this view of Caracas, the capital of Venezuela. Caracas is one of Latin America's most modern cities.*

Brazil is famous for growing coffee. Cocoa, soya beans and sugar cane are also important crops. Coal, iron ore and other minerals are abundant in Brazil. To the northeast of Brazil is Venezuela. Here rain forests also cover much of the land. Venezuela is a very rich country because it has valuable oilfields and iron ore. The money received from selling oil provides Venezuelans with factories, modern homes and roads.

Guyana, Surinam and French Guiana were once colonies of the British, Dutch and French. In these countries much of the land is covered with dense tropical forest and most people live in cities along the coast.

0   800 kms
0   500 miles

TOBAGO
TRINIDAD

⊙Maracaibo
Lake Maracaibo
☐Caracas
VENEZUELA

ATLANTIC OCEAN

R. Orinoco

▲ 5007m

R. Caroni
Angel Falls
Georgetown
GUYANA
• Paramaribo
☐ Cayenne
SURINAM
FRENCH GUIANA

COLOMBIA

Guiana Highlands

ADOR

R. Negro

• Manaus
• Belém
São Luis

R. Amazon
•Fortaleza

R. Purus
R. Madeira
R. Tapajós
BRAZIL
• João Pessoa
• Recife
• Maceió

PERU

Mato Grosso
R. Xingu
R. Tocantins
R. São Francisco
⊙Salvador

R. Paraguay

BOLIVIA
Goiania •
• Brasilia
Brazilian Highlands

PACIFIC
OCEAN
PARAGUAY

R. Parana
⊙ Belo Horizonte
▲ 2890m

Santos
• Rio de Janeiro
• Curitiba
⊙São Paulo

⊙Porto Alegre

URUGUAY

LEFT: *The spectacular Iguacu Falls form part of the border between Brazil and Argentina.*

Argentina and its Neighbours

Argentina

Chile

Paraguay

Uruguay

The countries of southern South America enjoy a mild climate, unlike their neighbours in the tropical north. The southern tip of the continent is very cool because it is not far from the frozen wastes of Antarctica.

Chile is long and narrow. In the north is the Atacama Desert, where workers mine copper, nitrates and iron ore. Many people in Chile try to live off the land, but farming is hard in most areas. People are leaving their farms to work in cities, such as Santiago.

Argentina is the second largest and the richest of all South American countries. Farmers rear sheep and cattle, and grow wheat, sugar cane and cotton on the fertile pampas or grasslands. Factory workers in the cities process these products. The production of steel, plastics, motor vehicles, oil and gas are also important.

Most people living in Chile and Argentina are descendants of the Spanish and are Spanish speaking. People from Europe, especially from Italy, are still going to live in these countries today.

ABOVE: *The Casa Rosada (pink house) in Buenos Aires houses the government of Argentina. Argentina became an independent country in 1816 after 300 years of Spanish rule.*

LEFT: *Snow covers the peaks of the Pine Horn Mountains in Torres del Paine National Park, Chile.*

BOLIVIA

BRAZIL

Arica
Iquique

Atacama Desert

Chiquicamata

PARAGUAY

ntofagasta

CHILE

Gran Chaco

Asunción

CIFIC
EAN

Andes Mountains

▲ Salado
6885m

Tucumán

R. Salado

R. Parana

R. Uruguay

Córdoba

Santa Fé

URUGUAY

Aconcagua
raiso
antiago
6960m

San Juan

Mendoza

Rosario

cepción

Talca

ARGENTINA

Pampas

Buenos Aires

Montevideo

La Plata

muco
divia

R. Colorado

Bahia Blanca

Mar del Plata

R. Negro

o Montt

ATLANTIC OCEAN

0   400 kms

0   200 miles

Comodoro Rivadavia

Patagonia

FALKLAND ISLANDS
(Britain)

Rio Gallegos

Punta Arenas

TIERRA DEL
FUEGO

Cape Horn

North Africa

Algeria

Chad

The vast Sahara Desert covers almost all of northern Africa. It is the largest, hottest desert in the world, stretching for 4800 kilometres from the Atlantic Ocean to the Red Sea. In the northwest, in Morocco and Algeria, lie the rugged Atlas Mountains.

ABOVE: *A Berber woman prepares her produce to sell at a market. She is wearing traditional Berber clothing.*

Egypt

Ethiopia

Libya

Mali

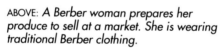

Mauritania

The people of northern Africa are mostly Muslim Arabs and Berbers who earn their living from farming. They live in river valleys and around oases, because there is no water in other areas. In Egypt it scarcely ever rains, except along the Mediterranean coast. Most farmers rely on the river Nile for water. The Aswan High Dam, built on the Nile in 1970, stores water for use during dry periods.

Tourists travel to Tunisia and Morocco every year to enjoy sunbathing on the beaches and wandering through the colourful bazaars, or markets. But many more tourists visit Egypt to see the pyramids at Giza – one of the seven wonders of the ancient world.

RIGHT: *Sand dunes in the Sahara. It is the world's largest desert and is slowly taking over more land southwards. Although it is extremely hot by day the temperature often falls to near freezing at night.*

ATLANTIC OCEAN Tangier
Rabat Fez
Casablanca
MADEIRA (Portugal) Marrakech MOROCCO Atlas Mou
CANARY ISLANDS (Spain)
Laayonne ALGE
WESTERN SAHARA
MAURITANIA M
Nouakchott
R. Senegal
SENEGAL
Timbukt
Bamako R. Niger BU
GUINEA F

0   800 kms
0   500 miles

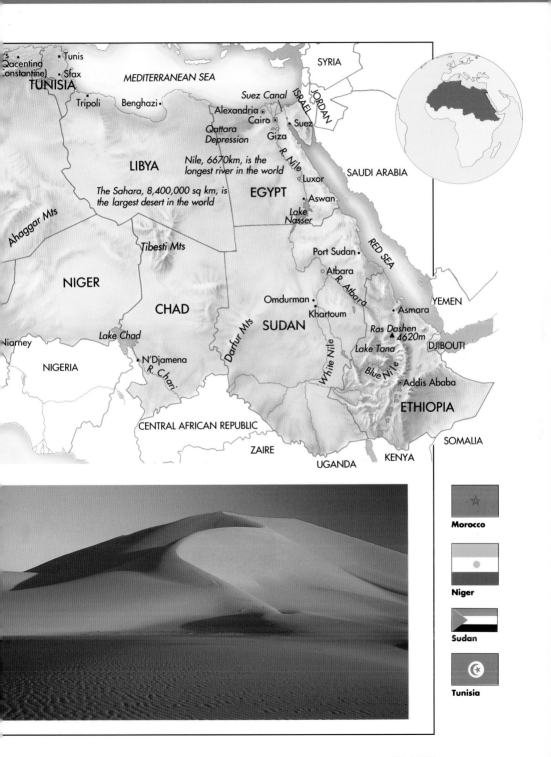

s •
Qacentina)
onstantine) • Sfax
• Tunis

TUNISIA

MEDITERRANEAN SEA

SYRIA

JORDAN

ISRAEL

Tripoli • Benghazi •

Suez Canal

Alexandria ◎
Cairo ⊡

• Suez

*Qattara
Depression*

Giza

R. Nile

SAUDI ARABIA

LIBYA

Nile, 6670km, is the
longest river in the world

• Luxor

EGYPT

The Sahara, 8,400,000 sq km, is
the largest desert in the world

• Aswan

*Lake
Nasser*

Ahaggar Mts

RED SEA

Tibesti Mts

Port Sudan •

NIGER

◎ Atbara

R. Atbara

YEMEN

CHAD

Omdurman •

Khartoum •

• Asmara

Ras Dashen
▲ 4620m

SUDAN

Darfur Mts

DJIBOUTI

Niamey •

Lake Chad

Lake Tana

White Nile

Blue Nile

⊡ Addis Ababa

NIGERIA

• N'Djamena

R. Chari

ETHIOPIA

CENTRAL AFRICAN REPUBLIC

SOMALIA

ZAIRE

UGANDA

KENYA

Morocco

Niger

Sudan

Tunisia

West Africa

West Africa is a jigsaw puzzle of countries. Many different groups of Black Africans live there. Nigeria alone has 250 groups. The people speak a number of African languages including Swahili. But official languages are often English, French or Portuguese because most of these countries were once ruled by these European nations.

The countries along the coast are hot and have long wet seasons. They are largely covered by tropical forest. Cocoa, coffee, palm oil and rubber are important crops. Root crops of cassava and yams provide food. Inland, on savanna grasslands, crops consist of cotton and groundnuts. Millet, maize and sorghum are grown for food. Cattle are kept for their meat as well as for their hides.

West African countries are building up their industries. There are new factories in Nigeria and Senegal, metals are mined in Sierra Leone and Ghana, and oil is drilled in Nigeria. The money received from exporting crops and minerals is used to build modern towns, schools and hospitals. But many of the people still live on the land just as their families have lived for centuries.

Benin

Burkino Faso

Cameroon

Congo

Côte d'Ivoire

Equatorial Guinea

Gabon

ABOVE LEFT: *Lengths of boldly patterned cloth such as this woman is carrying are used to make traditional clothing in West Africa.*

ABOVE: *Workers in a car manufacturing plant in Lagos, Nigeria. Many Nigerians have given up farming to work in industry.*

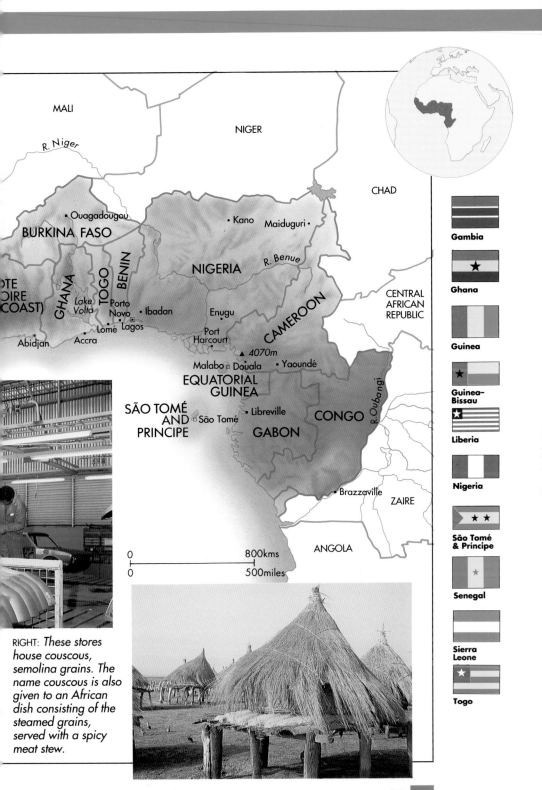

MALI

NIGER

R. Niger

CHAD

· Ouagadougou

BURKINA FASO

· Kano   Maiduguri ·

NIGERIA

R. Benue

TE
OIRE
COAST)

GHANA

TOGO

BENIN

Lake
Volta

Porto
Novo

· Ibadan

Enugu ·

CAMEROON

CENTRAL
AFRICAN
REPUBLIC

Lomé Lagos

Port
Harcourt

▲ 4070m

Abidjan Accra

Malabo · Douala · Yaoundé

EQUATORIAL
GUINEA

R. Oubangi

SÃO TOMÉ
AND
PRINCIPE

São Tomé

· Libreville

CONGO

GABON

· Brazzaville

ZAIRE

0 _____ 800kms
0 _____ 500miles

ANGOLA

Gambia

Ghana

Guinea

Guinea–
Bissau

Liberia

Nigeria

São Tomé
& Príncipe

Senegal

Sierra
Leone

Togo

RIGHT: *These stores
house couscous,
semolina grains. The
name couscous is also
given to an African
dish consisting of the
steamed grains,
served with a spicy
meat stew.*

55

Central and East Africa

Burundi

C. African Republic

Djibouti

Much of Central Africa is lowland covered with thick tropical forest. One of the greatest rivers in Africa, the river Zaire, runs through the region and is important for transport. Most people in Central Africa live in small clearings growing food crops such as yams and cassava. Sometimes parts of the forest are cleared for timber. Cocoa, coffee, palm oil and rubber are also important. Zaire's main source of wealth comes from copper mines in the southeastern part of the country.

LEFT: *Mount Kenya is an extinct volcano in central Kenya. At 5199 metres high it is the second tallest mountain in Africa, after Mount Kilimanjaro.*

Kenya

Rwanda

Somalia

Tanzania

East Africa is a region of highland and savanna grassland. A cool climate is typical of the East African plateau. In the past Europeans settled in this area, growing tea, coffee, cotton and sisal. Food crops consist of millet, maize and plantains.

Tourists often travel to Kenya to see wild animals. Once hunted, many lions, elephants, zebras and rhinos now live on large game reserves. Most of the people of Kenya belong to one of a number of different tribes, such as the Masai.

Somalia and Djibouti are mostly desert. The people living in these countries are animal herders and are often very poor.

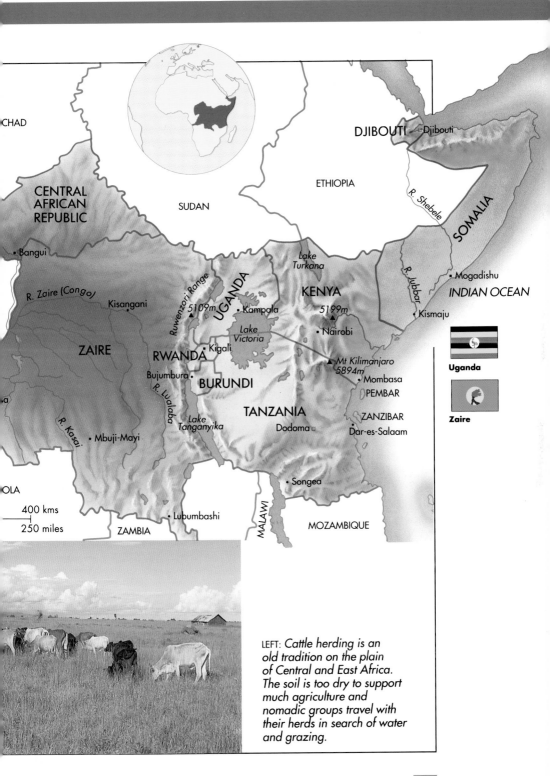

CHAD

DJIBOUTI — Djibouti

ETHIOPIA

CENTRAL
AFRICAN
REPUBLIC

SUDAN

R. Shebele

SOMALIA

• Bangui

Lake
Turkana

Ruwenzori Range

R. Zaire (Congo)

Kisangani

5109m
UGANDA

• Kampala

KENYA

5199m

R. Jubba

• Mogadishu

INDIAN OCEAN

ZAIRE

RWANDA

Kigali

Lake
Victoria

• Nairobi

• Kismaju

Bujumbura

BURUNDI

Mt Kilimanjaro
5894m

• Mombasa

Uganda

R. Lualaba

R. Kasai

• Mbuji-Mayi

Lake
Tanganyika

TANZANIA

Dodoma

PEMBAR

ZANZIBAR

Dar-es-Salaam

Zaire

OLA

• Songea

400 kms

250 miles

• Lubumbashi

ZAMBIA

MALAWI

MOZAMBIQUE

LEFT: *Cattle herding is an
old tradition on the plain
of Central and East Africa.
The soil is too dry to support
much agriculture and
nomadic groups travel with
their herds in search of water
and grazing.*

57

Southern Africa

Angola

Botswana

Comoros

Lesotho

Madagascar

Malawi

Mozambique

Southern Africa is very different from the rest of Africa. To start with its climate is cooler. Look for the Namib and Kalahari deserts on the map. Unlike the almost barren Sahara in northern Africa, the Kalahari is a dry, bush-covered plateau.

Many Europeans also live in this part of Africa. Large numbers of them first arrived in South Africa during the 1880s, attracted by the discovery of gold. Many stayed to farm the land or run mines and businesses.

South Africa and Zimbabwe are the richest countries in southern Africa. People from poorer countries, such as Botswana and Lesotho, often go to work in their large manu-facturing industries. South Africa produces a huge share of the world's gold and diamonds. Zimbabwe is also rich in mineral resources, including gold, asbestos, nickel and coal, but most people work in agriculture. There are large cattle ranches as well as maize, cotton, and tobacco farms.

In South Africa the government policy called apartheid, which has kept European and Black Africans apart, is beginning to be changed. Europeans still control the government and own the major businesses.

Madagascar is one of the largest islands in the world. It has many kinds of plants and animals which are found nowhere else in the world. Most of the people are farmers.

ABOVE: *Elephants roam freely in the Kruger National Park in South Africa. Several countries in southern Africa have established game reserves in order to protect their wildlife*

OPPOSITE: *South Africa's many gold mines produce half of the world's supply of the precious metal.*

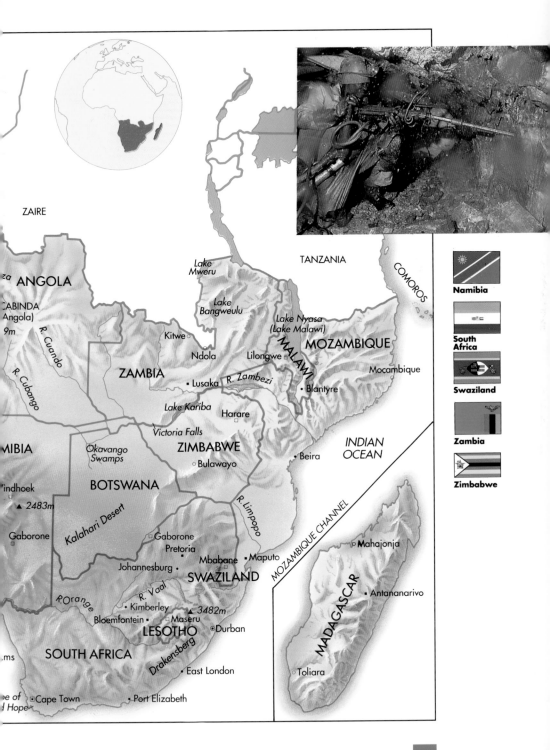

ZAIRE

ANGOLA

CABINDA
(Angola)
9m

R. Cuando

R. Cubango

za

Lake
Mweru

TANZANIA

COMOROS

Lake
Bangweulu

Lake Nyasa
(Lake Malawi)

MOZAMBIQUE

Kitwe •

Ndola •

Lilongwe •

MALAWI

Moçambique •

ZAMBIA

• Lusaka   R. Zambezi

• Blantyre

Lake Kariba

Harare •

Victoria Falls

ZIMBABWE

INDIAN
OCEAN

MIBIA

Okavango
Swamps

○ Bulawayo

• Beira

indhoek

BOTSWANA

▲ 2483m

Kalahari Desert

R. Limpopo

MOZAMBIQUE CHANNEL

Gaborone

□ Gaborone

Pretoria •

Johannesburg •

R. Vaal

• Mbabane • Maputo

MADAGASCAR

• Mahajonja

R. Orange

• Kimberley   ▲ 3482m

SWAZILAND

• Antananarivo

Bloemfontein • □ Maseru

LESOTHO

◉ Durban

ms

SOUTH AFRICA

Drakensberg

• East London

• Toliara

pe of
d Hope

□ Cape Town

• Port Elizabeth

Namibia

**South
Africa**

Swaziland

Zambia

Zimbabwe

Australia

Australia is the largest island and smallest continent in the world. It is sometimes called 'Down Under' because it lies south of the Equator among a group of islands in the Indian and Pacific Oceans.

Australia was discovered by Dutch sailors in the early 1600s. Much later in 1770, Captain Cook took possession of parts of eastern Australia for Britain. At that time the Aborigines were the only people living there. Later, in the 1850s gold was discovered and large numbers of settlers arrived from Europe in a hurry to make their fortunes. Today, besides gold, there are silver, copper, iron, zinc and aluminium mines.

LEFT: *Sydney is the capital of New South Wales and the largest city in Australia. The Sydney Opera House stands at the mouth of the harbour. Its roofs were designed to look like the sails of ships billowing in the wind.*

Much of the west of Australia is desert. Although it is a big country it is not very crowded. Most people live in cities along the cooler southeast coast. In the dry, central plains called the 'Outback', there are sheep and cattle stations. Sheep are kept mainly for their good quality wool which is sold to several other countries.

Port Hed
Dampier
R. Ashburton
▲ Mt Bruce
1227m
Carnavon   R. Gascoyne
R. Murchison
Geraldton
INDIAN
OCEAN   Wanneroo
Perth ★
Fremantle
Darling Range
Albany
W

ARAFURA SEA

MELVILLE I.

Darwin
Arnhem Land
R. Daly
R. Roper

GULF OF
CARPENTARIA

Cape York
Peninsula

PACIFIC OCEAN

OR SEA

R. Ord

R. Victoria

Sandy Desert

Tennant Creek

NORTHERN TERRITORY

R. Georgina

R. Leichhardt

R. Mitchell

Cairns

GREAT BARRIER REEF

R. Flinders

Townsville

Mount Isa

on Desert

Macdonnell Range
1524m ▲

Alice Springs

Rockhampton

Ayers Rock
▲ 867m

Simpson Desert

R. Diamantina

Great Dividing Range

STRALIA

Musgrave Ranges

AUSTRALIA

QUEENSLAND

Gold
Coast

R. Cooper

Toowoomba ○

★ Brisbane
• Southport

Victoria Desert

Lake
Eyre

SOUTH AUSTRALIA

orlie

Lake
Torrens

R. Darling

Nullabor Plain

Eucla

Broken Hill

NEW SOUTH WALES

• Newcastle

Flinders Ranges

Whyalla

GREAT AUSTRALIAN BIGHT

R. Murray

R. Murrumbidgee

Parramatta
• Sydney

Canberra

Port Lincoln ○

Adelaide ★

• Wollongong

R. Murray

Australian Alps

KANGAROO I.

VICTORIA

TASMAN
SEA

0   400 kms

0   200 miles

Ballarat ○

★ Melbourne

Geelong

LEFT: *Ayers Rock in the
Northern Territory is the
largest solitary rock mound in
the world. It is 335 metres
high and measures 10
kilometres around its base.
The Aborigines believe it is
a sacred place.*

KING I.

FLINDERS I.

Launceston ○

TASMANIA

Hobart ★

61

New Zealand and the Pacific

Fiji

Kiribati

Nauru

New Zealand and the thousands of islands of the Pacific Ocean are divided into three groups – Melanesia, Micronesia and Polynesia – according to the type of people who live on the islands. Kiribati, the Mariana Islands and the Caroline Islands form part of Micronesia, but Fiji and Papua New Guinea are included in Melanesia.

New Zealand is part of Polynesia because the Maoris, who are the original inhabitants, are Polynesian people. New Zealand has two main islands, North Island and South Island. In the 1800s, settlers arrived from Britain to farm and to prospect for gold. Today most people live in towns and cities, and the largest city is Auckland. But New Zealand remains a rich farming country. Dairy farming is very important and there are over nine million cattle and 55 million sheep. Many factory workers process meat, butter, cheese and milk.

New Zealand

Papua New Guinea

Solomon Islands

ABOVE: *New Zealand has plenty of good grazing land for the millions of sheep that it rears for meat and wool.*

Life on the Pacific Islands is often relaxed and simple. Many Pacific Islanders live in small villages. They grow food in gardens and fish skilfully from canoes. People on the larger islands often work on banana, coconut and cocoa plantations. Few of the islands have mineral resources, but phosphates have been heavily mined on Nauru, and there are copper mines on Bougainville, one of the tiny islands that belongs to Papua New Guinea.

Tonga

Tuvalu

NORTHERN MARIANA ISLANDS

PALAU (Trust T

IRIAN JAYA (INDONESIA)

AUSTRA

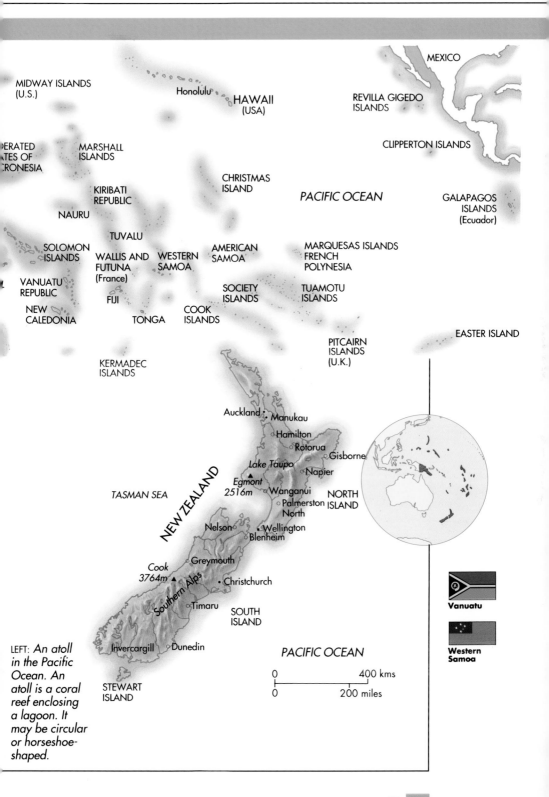

MIDWAY ISLANDS
(U.S.)

Honolulu

HAWAII
(USA)

MEXICO

REVILLA GIGEDO
ISLANDS

CLIPPERTON ISLANDS

ERATED
TES OF
RONESIA

MARSHALL
ISLANDS

CHRISTMAS
ISLAND

PACIFIC OCEAN

GALAPAGOS
ISLANDS
(Ecuador)

KIRIBATI
REPUBLIC

NAURU

TUVALU

SOLOMON
ISLANDS

WALLIS AND
FUTUNA
(France)

WESTERN
SAMOA

AMERICAN
SAMOA

MARQUESAS ISLANDS
FRENCH
POLYNESIA

VANUATU
REPUBLIC

FIJI

SOCIETY
ISLANDS

TUAMOTU
ISLANDS

NEW
CALEDONIA

TONGA

COOK
ISLANDS

EASTER ISLAND

PITCAIRN
ISLANDS
(U.K.)

KERMADEC
ISLANDS

Auckland   Manukau

Hamilton

Rotorua

Gisborne

Lake Taupo

Napier

Egmont
2516m

Wanganui

Palmerston
North

NORTH ISLAND

NEW ZEALAND

TASMAN SEA

Nelson

Wellington

Blenheim

Cook
3764m

Greymouth

Southern Alps

Christchurch

Timaru

SOUTH
ISLAND

Invercargill

Dunedin

PACIFIC OCEAN

STEWART
ISLAND

LEFT: *An atoll
in the Pacific
Ocean. An
atoll is a coral
reef enclosing
a lagoon. It
may be circular
or horseshoe-
shaped.*

0   400 kms
0   200 miles

Vanuatu

Western
Samoa

63

The Arctic and the Antarctic

PACIFIC OCEAN

ALASKA
(USA)

BERING STRAIT

EAST
SIBERIAN
SEA

for
US

BEAUFORT
SEA

NEW
SIBERIAN LAPTEV
ISLANDS SEA

CANADA

BANKS
ISLAND

VICTORIA I.

ARCTIC OCEAN

NORTH POLE

QUEEN
ELIZABETH
ISLANDS

HUDSON
BAY

ELLESMERE
ISLAND

FRANZ
JOSEF
LAND

BAFFIN ISLAND

Thule

NOVAYA
ZEMLYA

BAFFIN
BAY

SVALBARD
(NORWAY)

GREENLAND
(DENMARK)

BARENTS
SEA

Godthaab

GREENLAND
SEA

ATLANTIC
OCEAN

Hammerfest • Murmansk

LAPLAND

ARCTIC CIRCLE

ICELAND

NORWAY
SWEDEN
FINLAND

ABOVE: *Nomadic reindeer herders in Lapland.*

The area around the North Pole is called the Arctic. Much of it consists of the icy Arctic Ocean. But there are islands, including Greenland. Parts of North America, Europe and Asia also stretch beyond the Arctic Circle. The waters around the North Pole are frozen all the year round. But in other parts of the Arctic, the snow melts during the short summer weeks and patches of moss, lichen and bright flowers appear. The Inuit (Eskimos) and Lapps are the only people living in the Arctic. Most of the Inuit live on the southwest coast of Greenland and are skilled hunters and fishermen.

The continent of Antarctica covers more than 13 million square kilometres. It is larger than Europe and contains over 90 per cent of the world's ice and snow. It is so bitterly cold in Antarctica that no one has ever lived there permanently. Whalers went there in the 19th century, but they never left the safety of their ships. Since 1911, when Roald Amundsen first reached the South Pole, many scientists have been to the continent. They study the weather and the structure of the rocks buried in the ice. Some countries have built research stations there.

ABOVE: *Antarctic icebergs may be tens of kilometres across.*

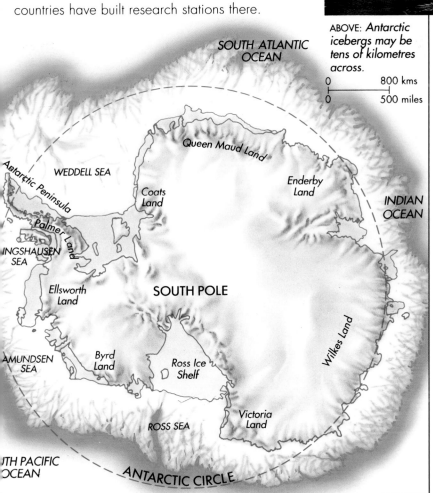

SOUTH ATLANTIC OCEAN

0   800 kms
0   500 miles

Queen Maud Land

WEDDELL SEA

Antarctic Peninsula

Enderby Land

Coats Land

INDIAN OCEAN

Palmer Land

BELLINGSHAUSEN SEA

Ellsworth Land

SOUTH POLE

AMUNDSEN SEA

Byrd Land

Ross Ice Shelf

Wilkes Land

Victoria Land

ROSS SEA

SOUTH PACIFIC OCEAN

ANTARCTIC CIRCLE

Facts and Figures

Europe

Country	Area (sq km)	Population	Capital	Official Language	Currency	Major Products
Albania	28,748	3,250,000	Tirana	Albanian	Lek	Oil, bitumen, metals (chrome, nickel,copper), tobacco, fruit and vegetables
Andorra	453	52,000	Andorra la Vella	Catalan, Spanish	French franc, peseta	Tourism, postage stamps
Austria	83,849	7,712,000	Vienna	German	Schilling	Food, iron and steel, textiles, paper products, machinery
Belgium	30,513	9,845,000	Brussels	Flemish, French	Belgian franc	Chemicals, vehicles, machinery,iron, steel
Bulgaria	110,912	9,011,000	Sofia	Bulgarian	Lev	Metals, machinery, textiles, tobacco, food
Czechoslo-vakia	127,869	15,662,000	Prague	Czech, Slovak	Koruna	Fuels, machinery, raw materials, manufactured goods,
Denmark	45,069	5,140,000	Copen-hagen	Danish	Krone	Animals, meat, dairy produce, eggs, machinery, metals and metal goods
Estonia	45,100	1,590,000	Tallin	Estonian, Russian	Rouble	Dairy products, fish, oil, textile (cotton), chemicals
Finland	337,009	4,986,000	Helsinki	Finnish, Swedish	Markka	Wood, paperboard, paper, paper machinery
France	547,026	55,000,000	Paris	French	French franc	Cars, electrical equipment, wine, textiles, chemicals, iron, steel
Germany	357,041	79,070,000	Berlin	German	Deutschmark	Engineering goods, coke manufactured goods, chemicals,
Greece	131,944	10,048,000	Athens	Greek	Drachma	Manufactured goods, food, animals, wine, tobacco
Hungary	93,030	10,553,000	Budapest	Magyar (Hungarian)	Florint	Transport equipment, bauxite, electrical goods, food, wine, pharmaceuticals
Iceland	103,000	255,000	Reykjavik	Icelandic	Krona	Fish products
Ireland, Republic of	70,285	3,557,000	Dublin	English, Irish	Irish pound (punt)	Meat and meat products, dairy products, beer, whiskey
Italy	301,252	57,663,000	Rome	Italian	Lira	Machinery, vehicles, iron, steel, textiles, footwear, plastics, fruit
Latvia	65,200	2,717,000	Riga	Latvian, Russian	Rouble	Dairy products, cattle, timber, machinery

Country	Area (sq km)	Population	Capital	Official Language	Currency	Major Products
Liechtenstein	157	29,000	Vaduz	German	Swiss franc	Cotton, screws, bolts, needles
Lithuania	65,200	3,728,000	Vilnius	Lithuanian, Russian	Rouble	Cereals, cattle, fish, plastics, ships, timber, machinery
Luxembourg	2,586	373,000	Luxembourg City	Letzeburgish, French	Luxembourg franc	Iron and steel, chemicals, vehicles, machinery
Malta	316	354,000	Valletta	Maltese, English	Maltese pound	Food, manufactured goods, ship repairing, tourism
Monaco	1.9	29,000	Monte Carlo	French	French franc	Tourism
Netherlands	40,844	14,700,000	Amsterdam; The Hague (Legislative)	Dutch	Guilder	Oil, chemicals, food and animals, machinery
Norway	324,219	4,242,000	Oslo	Norwegian	Krone	Animal products, paper, fish, metal products, metals, oil
Poland	312,677	38,186,000	Warsaw	Polish	Zloty	Lignite, coal, coke, iron and steel, ships, textiles, food
Portugal	92,082	10,525,000	Lisbon	Portuguese	Escudo	Textiles, timber, cork, wine chemicals, machinery, sardines
Romania	237,500	23,200,000	Bucharest	Romanian	Leu	Food, machinery, minerals, oil, metals, natural gas, chemicals
Russia	17,175,400	5,144,000	Moscow	Russian	Rouble	Wheat, sugar beet, timber, oil, minerals, coal, gas, textiles
San Marino	61	24,000	San Marino	Italian	Italian lira	Wine, cereals, cattle, tourism
Spain	504,782	38,959,000	Madrid	Spanish	Peseta	Manufactured goods, textiles, leather goods, wine, fruit, fish vegetables, olive oil
Sweden	449,964	8,559,000	Stockholm	Swedish	Swedish krona	Timber and timber products, cars, machinery, metals
Switzerland	41,288	6,500,000	Bern	German, French, Italian	Swiss franc	Tourism, machinery, chemicals watches, food, textiles
United Kingdom	244,828	57,237,000	London	English	Sterling pound	Electrical and engineering products, textiles, chemicals
Vatican City State	0.44	1,000	Vatican City	Latin, Italian	Italian lira	
Yugoslavia	255,804	23,898,000	Belgrade	Serbo-Croat, Slovene, Macedonian	Dinar	Machinery, electrical goods, transport equipment, chemicals

Facts and Figures

Asia

Country	Area (sq km)	Population	Capital	Official Language	Currency	Major Products
Afghanistan	652,092	16,121,000	Kabul	Pashtu, Dari (Persian)	Afghani	Skins, cotton, natural gas, fruit
Bahrain	668	503,000	Manama	Arabic	Dinar	Oil
Bangladesh	143,998	115,594,000	Dhaka	Bengali	Taka	Jute, leather, hide and skins, tea
Bhutan	47,000	1,517,000	Thimphu	Dzongkha, Nepali, English	Ngultrum	Rice, fruit, timber
Brunei	5,765	226,000	Bandar Seri Begawan	Malay	Brunei dollar	Oil
Cambodia	181,035	8,246,000	Phnom Penh	Khmer	Riel	Rice, rubber
China	9,596,961	1,070,600,000	Beijing	Chinese (Peking)	Yuan (Mandarin)	Industrial and agricultural products
Cyprus	9,251	702,000	Nicosia	Greek,	Pound Turkish	Fruit, vegetables, wine, manufactured goods, minerals
Hong Kong	1,046	5,801,000	Victoria	Chinese (Cantonese), English	Hong Kong dollar	Light manufactured goods, textiles, electronics
India	3,287,590	827,057,000	New Delhi	Hindi,	Rupee English	Tea, industrial goods, jute, textiles
Indonesia	2,027,087	179,300,000	Jakarta	Bahasa (Indonesian)	Rupiah	Oil, palm products, rubber, coffee
Iran	1,648,000	54,608,000	Tehran	Farsi (Persian)	Rial	Oil, natural gas, cotton
Iraq	434,924	18,920,000	Baghdad	Arabic	Iraqi dinar	Oil, dates, wool, cotton
Israel	20,770	4,659,000	Jerusalem	Hebrew, Arabic	Shekel	Cut diamonds, chemicals, fruit, tobacco
Japan	372,313	123,537,000	Tokyo	Japanese	Yen	Optical equipment, ships, vehicles, machinery, electronic goods, chemicals, textiles
Jordan	97,740	4,009,000	Amman	Arabic	Jordanian dinar	Phosphates, fruit, vegetables
Korea, North	120,538	21,773,000	Pyongyang	Korean	Won	Iron and other metal ores
Korea, South	98,484	42,793,000	Seoul	Korean	Won	Textiles, manufactured goods, chemicals
Kuwait	17,818	2,143,000	Kuwait City	Arabic	Kuwait dinar	Oil, chemicals

Country	Area (sq km)	Population	Capital	Official Language	Currency	Major Products
Laos	236,800	4,139,000	Vientiane	Lao	Kip	Timber, coffee
Lebanon	10,400	2,701,000	Beirut	Arabic	Lebanese pound	Precious metals, gemstones
Macao	17	430,000	Macao	Portuguese, Chinese	Pataca	Light manufactured goods
Malaysia	329,749	17,861,000	Kuala Lumpur	Malay	Malaysian dollar	Rubber, tin, palm oil, timber
Maldive Islands	298	215,000	Malé	Divehi	Rupee	Fish, copra
Mongolia	1,565,000	2,000,000	Ulan Bator	Mongolian	Tugrik	Cattle, horses, wool, hair
Myanmar (Burma)	676,552	41,675,000	Rangoon	Burmese	Kyat	Teak, oil cake, rubber, jute
Nepal	140,797	18,916,000	Katmandu	Nepali	Rupee	Grains, hides, cattle, timber
Oman	212,417	1,502,000	Muscat	Arabic	Omani riyal	Oil, dates, limes, tobacco, frankincense
Pakistan	803,943	112,050,000	Islamabad	Urdu, English	Rupee	Cotton, carpets, leather, rice
Philippines	300,000	62,000,000	Manila	Pilipino	Peso	Sugar, timber, coconut products
Qatar	11,000	368,000	Doha	Arabic	Qatar riyal	Oil
Saudi Arabia	2,149,690	14,870,000	Riyadh	Arabic	Riyal	Oil
Singapore	581	3,003,000	Singapore	Malay, Chinese, Tamil, English	Singapore dollar	Refined oil products, electronic goods, rubber
Sri Lanka	65,610	16,993,000	Colombo	Sinhala	Rupee	Tea, rubber, coconut products, industrial goods
Syria	185,180	12,116,000	Damascus	Arabic	Syrian pound	Cotton, oil, cereals, animals
Taiwan	35,961	20,280,000	Taipei	Chinese (Mandarin)	Taiwan dollar	Textiles, electrical goods, plastics, machinery, food
Thailand	514,000	55,000,000	Bangkok	Thai	Baht	Rice, tapioca, rubber, tin
Turkey	780,576	58,687,000	Ankara	Turkish	Turkish lira	Cotton, tobacco, nuts, fruit
United Arab Emirates	83,600	1,589,000	Abu Dhabi	Arabic	Dirham	Oil, natural gas
Vietnam	329,556	66,710,000	Hanoi	Vietnamese	Dong	Fish, coal, agricultural goods
Yemen	527,928	9,430,000	San'a	Arabic	Dinar	Cotton, coffee, hides and skins, fish, refined oil

Facts and Figures

North America

Country	Area (sq km)	Population	Capital	Official Language	Currency	Major Products
Antigua and Barbuda	442	77,000	St John's	English	East Caribbean dollar	Oil products
Bahamas	13,935	253,000	Nassau	English	Bahamian dollar	Oil products
Barbados	431	255,000	Bridgetown	English	East Caribbean dollar	Sugar, oil products, electrical goods, clothing
Belize	22,965	188,000	Belmopan	English, Spanish	Belize dollar	Sugar, bananas, fish, citrus products, clothing
Canada	9,976,130	26,522,000	Ottawa	English, French	Canadian dollar	Wheat, natural gas, oil, wood pulp, newsprint, iron ore, cars and parts, fish,
Costa Rica	50,700	2,994,000	San José	Spanish	Colon	Coffee, bananas, manufactured goods
Cuba	114,524	10,609,000	Havana	Spanish	Peso	Sugar, tobacco
Dominica	751	83,000	Roseau	English	East Caribbean dollar	Citrus fruits, bananas
Dominican Republic	48,734	7,170,000	Santo Domingo	Spanish	Peso	Sugar, coffee
El Salvador	21,041	5,000,000	San Salvador	Spanish	Colon	Coffee, cotton
Grenada	344	85,000	St George's	English	East Caribbean dollar	Cocoa, nutmeg, mace, bananas
Guatemala	108,889	9,197,000	Guatemala City	Spanish	Quetzal	Coffee, bananas, cotton, beef
Haiti	27,750	6,486,000	Port-au-Prince	French	Gourde	Coffee, bauxite, sugar
Honduras	112,088	5,105,000	Tegucigalpa	Spanish	Lempira	Coffee, bananas, timber, meat
Jamaica	10,991	2,420,000	Kingston	English	Jamaican dollar	Bauxite, alumina
Mexico	1,972,547	86,154,000	Mexico City	Spanish	Peso	Oil, coffee, cotton, sugar, manufactured goods
Nicaragua	130,000	3,871,000	Managua	Spanish	Cordoba	Cotton, coffee, meat, chemicals
Panama	75,650	2,418,000	Panama City	Spanish	Balboa	Bananas, shrimps, sugar, oil products

Country	Area (sq km)	Population	Capital	Official Language	Currency	Major Products
St Kitts-Nevis	262	44,000	Basseterre	English	East Caribbean dollar	Sugar
St Lucia	616	151,000	Castries	English	East Caribbean dollar	Fruit, cocoa, tourism, cocnuts, manufactured goods
St Vincent and the Grenadines	388	116,000	Kingstown	English	East Caribbean dollar	Bananas, arrowroot, coconuts
Trinidad and Tobago	5,130	1,300,000	Port of Spain	English	Trinidad dollar	Oil, asphalt, chemicals, fruit, cocoa, coffee, sugar,
United States	9,363,123	249,975,000	Washington DC	English	US Dollar	Machinery, vehicles, aircraft, iron and steel, coal, cereals, chemicals, soya beans

South America

Country	Area (sq km)	Population	Capital	Official Language	Currency	Major Products
Argentina	2,766,889	32,322,000	Buenos Aires	Spanish	Peso	Meat, tobacco, textiles, leather, machinery
Bolivia	1,093,581	7,400,000	La Paz (Legislative); Sucre (Legal)	Spanish	Peso	Tin, oil, natural gas, cotton
Brazil	8,511,965	150,368,000	Brasilia	Portuguese	Cruzeiro	Machinery, vehicles, soya beans, coffee, cocoa
Chile	765,945	13,173,000	Santiago	Spanish	Peso	Wood pulp, paper, copper, timber, iron ore, nitrates
Colombia	1,138,914	32,987,000	Bogotá	Spanish	Peso	Coffee, emeralds, sugar, oil, meat, skins and hides
Ecuador	283,561	10,782,000	Quito	Spanish	Sucre	Oil, bananas, cocoa, coffee
French Guiana	91,000	92,000	Cayenne	French	French franc	Bauxite, shrimps, bananas
Guyana	214,000	796,000	Georgetown	English	Guyanese dollar	Sugar, rice, bauxite, alumina, timber
Paraguay	406,752	4,277,000	Asunción	Spanish	Guarani	Cotton, soya beans, tobacco, timber
Peru	1,285,216	22,332,000	Lima	Spanish	Sol	Metals, minerals (silver, lead, copper), fish, zinc,
Surinam	163,265	422,000	Paramaribo	Dutch, English	Guilder	Bauxite, alumina, rice, fruit
Uruguay	176,216	3,094,000	Montevideo	Spanish	Peso	Meat, wool, hides and skins
Venezuela	912,050	19,700,000	Caracas	Spanish	Bolivar	Oil, iron, cocoa, coffee

Facts and Figures

Africa

Country	Area (sq km)	Population	Capital	Official Language	Currency	Major Products
Algeria	2,381,741	24,960,000	Algiers	Arabic	Algerian dinar	Natural gas, oil
Angola	1,246,700	10,020,000	Luanda	Portuguese	Kwanza	Coffee, diamonds, oil
Benin	112,522	4,736,000	Porto Novo	French	Franc CFA	Cocoa, cotton
Botswana	600,372	1,291,000	Gaborone	English, Setswana	Pula	Copper, diamonds, meat
Burkino Faso	274,200	9,001,000	Ouagadougou	French	Franc CFA	Livestock, groundnuts, cotton
Burundi	27,834	5,458,000	Bujumbura	French, Kirundi	Burundi franc	Coffee
Cameroon	475,442	11,834,000	Yaoundé	English, French	Franc CFA	Cocoa, coffee, oil
Cape Verde Islands	4,033	370,000	Praia	Portuguese	Escudo	Bananas, fish
Central African Republic	622,984	3,039,000	Bangui	French	Franc CFA	Coffee, diamonds, timber
Chad	1,284,000	5,679,000	N'Djamena	French	Franc CFA	Cotton, cattle, meat
Comoros	2,171	551,000	Moroni	French	Franc CFA	Spices
Congo	342,000	2,271,000	Brazzaville	French	Franc CFA	Oil, timber
Côte d'Ivoire (Ivory Coast)	322,463	11,998,000	Yamoussoukro	French	Franc CFA	Cocoa, coffee, timber
Djibouti	22,000	409,000	Djibouti	French	Djibouti franc	Cattle, hides and skins
Egypt	1,001,449	53,153,000	Cairo	Arabic	Egyptian pound	Cotton, oil, textiles
Equatorial Guinea	28,055	348,000	Malabo	Spanish	Ekuele	Cocoa, coffee, timber
Ethiopia	1,221,900	49,241,000	Addis Ababa	Amharic	Ethiopian dollar	Coffee, hides and skins
Gabon	267,667	1,069,000	Libreville	French	Franc CFA	Manganese, oil
Gambia	11,295	861,000	Banjul	English	Dalasi	Groundnuts
Ghana	238,537	15,028,000	Accra	English	Cedi	Cocoa, gold, timber
Guinea	245,957	5,756,000	Conakry	French	Syli	Alumina, bauxite
Guinea-Bissau	36,125	965,000	Bissau	Portuguese	Escudo	Fish, groundnuts

Country	Area (sq km)	Population	Capital	Official Language	Currency	Major Products
Kenya	582,646	24,032,000	Nairobi	English, Swahili	Kenya shilling	Coffee, tea, hides
Lesotho	30,355	1,774,000	Maseru	English, Sesotho	Loti	Wool, mohair
Liberia	111,369	2,607,000	Monrovia	English	Liberian dollar	Iron ore, rubber
Libya	1,759,540	4,545,000	Tripoli	Arabic	Libyan dinar	Oil
Madagascar	587,041	11,197,000	Antananarivo	French, Malagasy	Malgache franc	Coffee, spices, vanilla
Malawi	118,484	8,289,000	Lilongwe	English, Chichewa	Kwacha	Tobacco, tea
Mali	1,240,000	8,156,000	Bamako	French	Mali franc	Groundnuts, cotton
Mauritania	1,030,700	2,025,000	Nouakchott	Arabic, French	Ouguiya	Iron ore, copper
Mauritius	2,085	1,075,000	Port Louis	English	Rupee	Sugar, tea, tobacco
Morocco	446,550	25,061,000	Rabat	Arabic	Dirham	Phosphates, fruit
Mozambique	783,030	15,656,000	Maputo	Portuguese	Metical	Sugar, fruit, vegetables
Namibia	824,292	1,781,000	Windhoek	Afrikaans, English	Rand	Minerals, diamonds, fish
Niger	1,267,000	7,732,000	Niarney	French	Franc CFA	Groundnuts, livestock, uranium
Nigeria	923,768	108,542,000	Lagos	English	Naira	Oil, palm kernels, cocoa
Rwanda	26,338	7,181,000	Kigali	French, Kinyarwanda	Rwanda franc	Coffee
São Tomé and Principe	965	121,000	São Tomé	Portuguese	Dobra	Cocoa
Senegal	196,192	7,327,000	Dakar	French	Franc CFA	Groundnuts, phosphates
Seychelles	280	70,000	Victoria	English, French	Rupee	Copra, fish, spices
Sierra Leone	71,740	4,151,000	Freetown	English	Leone	Diamonds, iron ore
Somalia	637,657	7,497,000	Mogadishu	Somali	Somali shilling	Livestock
South Africa	1,221,037	35,282,000	Pretoria (Legislative); Cape Town (Legal)	Afrikaans, English	Rand	Gold, diamonds, fruit, vegetables

Facts and Figures

Country	Area (sq km)	Population	Capital	Official Language	Currency	Major Products
Sudan	2,505,813	25,204,000	Khartoum	Arabic	Sudanese pound	Cotton, groundnuts
Swaziland	17,363	748,000	Mbabane	English, Siswati	Lilangeni	Sugar, wood pulp, asbestos, fruit
Tanzania	945,087	25,635,000	Dodoma	English, Swahili	Tanzanian shilling	Coffee, cotton, sisal, spices
Togo	56,000	3,531,000	Lomé	French	Franc CFA	Phosphates, cocoa, coffee
Tunisia	163,610	8,180,000	Tunis	Arabic	Dinar	Phosphates, olive oil, oil
Uganda	236,036	18,795,000	Kampala	English	Ugandan shilling	Coffee, cotton
Zaire	2,345,409	35,562,000	Kinshasa	French	Zaire	Coffee, cobalt, copper
Zambia	752,614	8,073,000	Lusaka	English	Kwacha	Copper
Zimbabwe	390,580	9,369,000	Harare	English	Zimbabwe dollar	Tobacco

Oceania

Country	Area (sq km)	Population	Capital	Official Language	Currency	Major Products
Australia	7,686,849	17,086,000	Canberra	English	Australian dollar	Cereals, meat, sugar, honey, fruit, metals and mineral ores, wool
Fiji	18,274	765,000	Suva	English, Fijian	Fiji dollar	Sugar, coconut oil
Kiribati	931	66,000	Tarawa	English, Gilbertese	Australian dollar	Copra, phosphates, fish
Nauru	21	10,000	Nauru	English, Nauruan	Australian dollar	Phosphates
New Zealand	268,676	3,346,000	Wellington	English	NZ dollar	Meat, dairy products, wool, fruit
Papua New Guinea	461,691	3,699,000	Port Moresby	English	Kina	Copra, cocoa, coffee, copper
Soloman Islands	28,446	321,000	Honiara	English	Soloman Islands dollar	Timber, fish, copra, palm oil
Tonga	699	95,000	Nuku'alofa	English	Pa'anga	Copra, bananas
Tuvalu	25	10,000	Funafuti	English, Tuvalu	Australian dollar	Copra
Vanuatu	14,763	147,000	Port-Vila	Bislama, English, French	Vatu	Copra, fish
Western Samoa	2,842	200,000	Apia	English, Samoan	Tala	Copra, cocoa, bananas

Map Index

achen 19
alborg 13
are river 19
arhus 13
oadan 29
bidjan 55
bilene 41
bu Dhabi 5, 29
capulco 44
ccra 55
concagua 51
dana 29
ddis Ababa 53
delaide 61
den 29
den, Gulf of 29
driatic Sea 23, 25
egean Sea 23
fghanistan 5, 31
frica 6–7, 52–9
gra 31
haggar Mts 52–3
hamadabad 31
jaccio 25
mer 31
kita 35
abama 41
aska 4, 38, 40, 64
lbania 4, 23
lbany, Australia 60
lbany, USA 41
lbany river 39
lberta 38–9
lbufeira 17
lbuquerque 40
leppo 29
lexandria 53
lgarve Coast 17
lgeria 4, 52–3
lgiers 53
licante 17
lice Springs 61
llahabad 31
ller river 19
lma Ata 27
lmeria 17
lps 15, 19
ltai Mts 33
ltyn Tagh Mts 33
marillo 41
mazon river 47, 49
merica see Central America; North America; South America
merican Samoa 63
miens 15
mman 29
mritsar 31
msterdam 11
mundsen Sea 65
mur river 26
nchorage 41
ndalucia 17
ndaman Islands 37
ndes Mts 47, 51
ndorra 17

Andorra la Vella 17
Angel Falls 49
Angers 15
Angola 5, 59
Ankara 29
Annapolis 41
Anshan 33
Antananarivo 59
Antarctica 65
Antarctic Circle 65
Antarctic Peninsula 65
Antigua and Barbuda 45
Antilles 45
Antofagasta 51
Antwerp 11
Aomori 35
Apajos river 49
Apeldoorn 11
Apennines 25
Appalachian Mts 41
Arabian Sea 29, 31
Arafura Sea 60–1
Aral Sea 26
Ararat, Mt 29
Arctic 64
Arctic Circle 64
Arctic Ocean 6–7, 13, 26, 64
Ardennes 11
Arequipa 47
Argentina 4, 51
Arica 51
Arizona 40
Arkansas 41
Arkansas river 40–1
Arkhangelsk 26
Arles 15
Armenia 26
Arnhem 11
Arnhem Land 61
Asahigawa 35
Ashburton river 60
Asia 7, 27–37
Askhabad 26
Asmara 53
Assisi 25
Astrakhan 26
Asunción 51
Aswan 53
Atacama Desert 51
Atbara 53
Atbara river 53
Athabaska, Lake 38–9
Athens 23
Atlanta 41
Atlantic Ocean 6
Atlas Mts 52
Auckland 63
Augsburg 19
Augusta 41
Austin 41
Australia 5, 60–1, 62
Australian Alps 61
Austria 4, 19
Avignon 15
Avon river 9
Ayers Rock 61

Ayr 9
Azerbaijan 26

Baffin Bay 39, 64
Baffin Island 39, 64
Baghdad 29
Bahamas 4, 45
Bahia Blanca 51
Bahrain 4, 29
Baikal, Lake 26
Baja California 44
Baku 26
Balaton, Lake 21
Balearic Islands 17
Bali 37
Balkan Mts 23
Balkans 23
Balkhash, Lake 27
Ballarat 61
Baltic Sea 13, 19
Baltimore 41
Bamako 52
Bandar Seri Begawan 37
Banda Sea 37
Bandjarmasin 37
Bandung 37
Bangalore 31
Bangkok 37
Bangladesh 5, 31
Bangor 41
Bangui 57
Bangweulu, Lake 59
Banjul 54
Banks Island 39, 64
Baotou 33
Barbados 4, 45
Barbuda see Antigua and Barbuda
Barcelona 17
Barents Sea 64
Bari 25
Barranquilla 47
Barrow river 9
Basel 19
Basra 29
Bath 9
Baton Rouge 41
Bayonne 15
Beaufort Sea 38–9, 64
Begawan 37
Beijing 33
Beira 59
Beirut 29
Belem 49
Belfast 9
Belgium 4, 11
Belgrade 23
Belize 5, 45
Bellingshausen Sea 65
Belmopan 45
Belo Horizonte 49
Benares 31
Bendigo 61
Bengal, Bay of 31
Benghazi 53

Benguela 59
Benin 4, 55
Beni river 47
Benue river 55
Bergen 13
Bering Strait 64
Berlin 19
Berne 19
Besancon 15
Bhopal 31
Bhutan 5, 31
Bialystok 21
Biarritz 15
Bielefeld 19
Bilbao 17
Billings 40
Birmingham, England 9
Birmingham, USA 41
Biscay, Bay of 15, 25
Bismarck 41
Bissau 54
Black Forest 19
Blackpool 9
Black Sea 26, 29
Blanc, Mt 15
Blantyre 59
Blenheim 63
Bloemfontein 59
Blue Nile river 53
Bochum 19
Bodensee 19
Bogota 47
Boise 40
Bolivia 4, 47
Bologna 25
Bolzano 25
Bombay 31
Bonn 19
Boras 13
Bordeaux 15
Bosnia Herzegovina 23
Boston 41
Bothnia, Gulf of 13
Botswana 5, 59
Boulogne 15
Bourgogne 15
Bournemouth 9
Bradford 9
Braga 17
Brahmaputra river 31, 33
Brandon 39
Brasilia 49
Brasov 23
Bratislava 21
Brazil 4, 49
Brazilian Highlands 49
Brazzaville 55
Breda 11
Bremen 19
Bremerhaven 19
Brescia 25
Brest 15
Brighton 9
Brindisi 25

Brisbane 61
Bristol 9
British Columbia 38
British Isles 9
Brno 21
Broken Hill 61
Broome 60
Bruce, Mt 60
Bruges 11
Brunei 37
Brunswick 19
Brussels 11
Bucaramanga 47
Bucharest 23
Budapest 21
Buenos Aires 51
Buffalo 41
Bug river 21
Bujumbura 57
Bukhara 27
Bulawayo 59
Bulgaria 5, 23
Burgas 23
Burgos 17
Burgundy 15
Burkina Faso 5, 55
Burma see Myanmar
Burundi 5, 57
Bydgoszcz 21
Byelorussia 26
Byrd Land 65

Cabinda 59
Cadiz 17
Caen 15
Cagliari 25
Cairns 61
Cairo 53
Calais 15
Calcutta 31
Calgary 38
Cali 47
Calicut 31
California 40
California, Gulf of 44
Callao 47
Camaguey 45
Cambodia 5, 37
Cambrian Mts 9
Cambridge 9
Cameroon 5, 55
Canada 4, 38–9, 64
Canary Islands 52
Canberra 61
Cancer, Tropic of 4–5, 6–7
Cannes 15
Canterbury 9
Canton see Guangzhou
Cape Canaveral 41
Cape Cod 41
Cape of Good Hope 59
Cape Horn 51
Cape Town 59
Cape Verde Islands 4

Cape York Peninsula 61
Capri 25
Capricorn, Tropic of 4–5, 6–7
Caracas 49
Carcassonne 15
Cardiff 9
Caribbean Sea 45
Carnarvon 60
Caroline Islands 62
Caroni river 49
Carpathian Mts 21, 23
Carpentaria, Gulf of 61
Carson City 41
Cartagena, Colombia 47
Casablanca 52
Cascade Range 40–1
Casper 40
Caspian Sea 26, 29
Catania 25
Caucasus Mts 26
Cayenne 49
Cebu 37
Celebes see Sulawesi
Celebes Sea 37
Central Africa 57
Central African Republic 5, 57
Central America 6, 44–5
Ceram 37
Cevennes Mts 15
Chad 5, 53
Chad, Lake 53
Champagne 15
Chang Jiang river 33
Changsha 33
Channel Islands 9, 15
Chao Phraya river 37
Chari river 53
Charleroi 11
Charleston, South Carolina 41
Charleston, West Virginia 41
Charlotte 41
Charlottetown 39
Chartres 15
Chattanooga 51
Chelyabinsk 27
Chengdu 33
Cherbourg 15
Cheyenne 41
Chiba 35
Chicago 41
Chiclayo 47
Chihuahua 44
Chile 4, 51
Chiltern Hills 9
Chimbote 47

Map Index

China 33
Chiquicamata 51
Chittagong 31
Chongqing 33
Christchurch 63
Christmas Island 63
Churchill 39
Churchill river 39
Cienfuegos 45
Cincinnati 41
Clermont-Ferrand 15
Cleveland 41
Clipperton Islands 63
Cluj 23
Clyde river 9
Coast Ranges 40
Coats Land 65
Cochabamba 47
Cochin 31
Coimbra 17
Cologne 19
Colombia 4, 47
Colombo 31
Colorado 40-1
Colorado river, Argentina 51
Colorado river, USA 41
Colorado Springs 41
Columbia 41
Columbia river 40
Columbus, Georgia 41
Columbus, Ohio 41
Comodoro Rivadavia 51
Como, Lake 25
Comoros 59
Conakry 54
Concepcion 51
Concord 41
Congo 5, 55
Congo river see Zaire river
Connecticut 41
Constance, Lake 19
Constanta 23
Constantine see Qacentina
Continents 6-7
Cook, Mt 63
Cook Islands 63
Cooper river 61
Copenhagen 13
Coral Sea 62
Cordoba, Argentina 51
Cordoba, Spain 17
Corfu 23
Corinth 23
Cork 9
Corpus Christi 41
Corsica 25
Costa Rica 5, 45
Côte d'Ivoire 4, 54-5
Cotswolds 9
Cottbus 19
Coventry 9

Craiova 23
Crete 23
Croatia 23
Cuando river 59
Cuanza river 59
Cuba 4, 45
Cubango river 59
Culiacan 44
Cunene river 59
Curitiba 49
Cuttack 31
Cuzco 47
Cyprus 4, 29
Czechoslovakia 4, 21

Dakar 54
Dalian 33
Dallas 41
Dal river 13
Daly river 61
Damascus 29
Dampier 60
Da Nang 37
Danube river 19, 21, 23
Dar-es-Salaam 57
Darfur Mts 53
Darjeeling 31
Darling Range 61
Darling river 61
Darmstadt 19
Dartmoor 9
Darwin 61
Davao 37
Davenport 41
Dawson 38
Dead Sea 29
Debrecen 23
Deccan Plateau 31
Dee river 9
Delaware 41
Delhi 31
Delphi 23
Denmark 4, 13
Denver 41
Derg, Lough 9
Des Moines 41
Dessau 19
Detroit 41
Devon Island 39
Dhaka 31
Diamantina river 61
Dieppe 15
Dijon 15
Dinaric Alps 23
Djibouti 5, 57
Dnieper river 26
Dodoma 57
Doha 29
Dominica 4, 45
Dominican Republic 5, 45
Donetsk 26
Don river 26
Dordogne river 15
Dordrecht 11
Dore, Mt 15
Dortmund 19
Douai 15
Douala 55

Douro river 17
Dover, England 9
Dover, USA 41
Drakensberg 59
Drava river 23
Dresden 19
Dubai 29
Dublin 9
Dubrovnik 23
Duero river 17
Duisburg 19
Dundee 9
Dunedin 63
Dunfermline 9
Dunkerque 15
Durban 59
Durres 23
Dusseldorf 19

East Africa 57
East China Sea 33
Easter Island 63
Eastern Europe 21
Eastern Ghats 31
East London 59
East Siberian Sea 26, 64
Ebro river 17
Ecuador 4, 47
Eden river 9
Edinburgh 9
Edmonton 38
EgmontMt 63
Egypt 5, 53
Eindhoven 11
Eire see Ireland, Republic of
Elbe river 19, 21
Elbrus, Mt 26
Elburz Mts 29
Ellesmere Island 64
Ellsworth Land 65
El Paso 40
El Salvador 5, 45
Ems river 19
Enderby Land 65
England 9
English Channel 9, 15
Enns river 19
Enschede 11
Enugu 55
Equator 4-5, 6-7
Equatorial Guinea 5, 55
Erfurt 19
Erie, Lake 39, 41
Eritrea 53
Esbjerg 13
Esfahan 29
Eskilstuna 13
Essen 19
Estonia 5, 26
Ethiopia 5, 53
Etna, Mt 25
Eucla 61
Euphrates river 29
Europe 6-7, 8-27
Evansville 41
Everest, Mt 31
Exeter 9

Exmoor 9
Eyre, Lake 61

Fairbanks 38
Faisalabad 31
Falkland Islands 4, 51
Faro 17
Fens 9
Ferrara 25
Fez 52
Fiji 5, 63
Finland 5, 13
Finland, Gulf of 13
Fishguard 9
Flinders Island 61
Flinders Ranges 61
Flinders river 61
Florence 25
Flores 37
Flores Sea 37
Florida 41
Florida, Straits of 45
Fontainebleau 15
Fortaleza 49
Fort Lauderdale 41
Fort Rupert 39
Fort Smith 41
Fort Worth 41
France 4, 15
Frankfort 41
Frankfurt 19
Franz Josef Land 26, 64
Fredericton 39
Freetown 54
Freiburg 19
Fremantle 60
French Guiana 5, 49
French Polynesia 63
Frisian Islands 11
Frunze 27
Fuji, Mt 35
Fukuoka 35
Fushun 33
Fuzhou 33

Gabon 5, 55
Gaborone 59
Galapagos Islands 63
Galati 23
Gallivare 13
Galway 9
Gambia 5, 54
Gambia river 54
Ganges river 31
Garda, Lake 25
Garonne river 15
Gascoyne river 60
Gavle 13
Gaza Strip 29
Gdansk 21
Geelong 61
Geneva 19
Geneva, Lake see Leman, Lake
Genoa 25
Georgetown 49
Georgia 26

Georgia, USA 41
Georgina river 61
Gera 19
Germany 4, 19
Ghana 4, 55
Ghent 11
Gibraltar 17
Gibson Desert 60-1
Gijon 17
Gisborne 63
Giza 53
Glama river 13
Glasgow 9
Glittertind, Mt 13
Glommen river 13
Goa 31
Gobi Desert 33
Godavari river 31
Godthaab 64
Goiania 49
Golan Heights 29
Gold Coast 61
Gorki 26
Goteborg 13
Gotland 13
Grampians 9
Granada 17
Gran Chaco 51
Grand Canyon 40
Grand Rapids 41
Graz 19
Great Australian Bight 60-1
Great Barrier Reef 61
Great Bear Lake 38-9
Great Dividing Range 59
Greater Antilles 45
Great Falls 40
Great Salt Desert 29
Great Salt Lake 40
Great Sand Desert 29
Great Sandy Desert 60-1
Great Slave Lake 38-9
Great Victoria Desert 60-1
Great Wall of China 33
Great Yarmouth 9
Greece 5, 23
Greenland 64
Greenland Sea 64
Grenada 45
Grenadines see St Vincent and the Grenadines
Grenoble 15
Greymouth 63
Groningen 11
Groote Eylandt 61
Gross Glockner 19
Guadalajara 44
Guadalquivir river 17
Guadeloupe 45
Guadiana river 17

Guangzhou 33
Guatemala 5, 45
Guatemala City 45
Guayaquil 47
Guiana Highlands 49
Guinea 5, 54
Guinea-Bissau 5, 54
Guiyang 33
Guyana 5, 49
Gyor 23

Haarlem 11
Hague, The 11
Hainan 33
Haiphong 37
Haiti 5, 45
Hakodate 35
Halab 29
Halifax 39
Halle 19
Halmahera 37
Halmstad 13
Halsingborg 13
Hamamatsu 35
Hamburg 19
Hamilton, Canada 39
Hamilton, New Zealand 63
Hammerfest 13
Hangzhou 33
Hanoi 37
Hanover 19
Harare 59
Harbin 33
Hardanger fiord 13
Harrisburg 41
Hartford 41
Harz Mts 19
Havana 45
Hawaii 40, 41
Hebrides 9
Heerlen-Kerkrase 11
Hekla, Mt 13
Helena 40
Helmand river 31
Helsinki 13
Herat 31
Hermosillo 44
Highlands, Scotland 9
Himalayas 31, 33
Hindu Kush 31
Hiroshima 35
Hobart 61
Ho Chi Minh City 37
Hohhot 33
Hokkaido 35
Holguin 45
Honduras 5, 45
Honduras, Gulf of 45
Hong Kong 5, 33
Honolulu 41
Honshu 35
Houston 41
Huambo 59
Huancayo 47
Huang He river 33

Hudson Bay 39, 64
Hudson Strait 39
Hue 37
Huelva 17
Hull 9
Hungary 4, 21
Huron, Lake 39, 41
Hyderabad 31

Iasi 23
Ibadan 55
Ibiza 17
Iceland 4, 13, 64
Idaho 40
IJsselmeer 11
IJssel river 11
Illinois 41
India 5, 31
Indiana 41
Indianapolis 41
Indian Ocean 6–7, 31, 37, 57, 59, 60, 65
Indonesia 5, 37
Indore 31
Indus river 31
Inn river 19
Innsbruck 19
Invercargill 63
Inverness 9
Ionian Sea 23
Iowa 41
Ipswich 9
Iquique 51
Iquitos 47
Iraklion 23
Iran 5, 29
Iraq 5, 29
Ireland, Northern 4, 9
Ireland, Republic of 4, 9
Irian Jaya 62
Irish Sea 9
Irkutsk 27
Irrawaddy river 37
Iskar river 23
Islamabad 31
Israel 4, 29
Issel river 11
Istanbul 29
Italy 4, 25
Ivory Coast see Côte d'Ivoire
Iwaki 35
Izmir 29

Jackson 41
Jacksonville 41
Jaipur 31
Jakarta 37
Jamaica 5, 45
Jammu and Kashmir 31
Japan 5, 35
Japan, Sea of 26, 35
Java 37
Java Sea 37
Jeddah 29
Jefferson City 41

Jerusalem 29
Jilin 33
Jinan 33
Joao Pessoa 49
Jodhpur 31
Johannesburg 59
Johnston Islands 63
Jonkoping 13
Jordan 4, 29
Juba river 57
Juneau 41
Jura Mts 15, 19
Jyvaskyla 13

Kabul 31
Kaduna 55
Kagoshima 35
Kaitaia 63
Kalahari Desert 59
Kalamata 23
Kalgoorlie 60
Kalimantan 37
Kamchatka Peninsula 27
Kampala 57
Kampuchea see Cambodia
Kanazawa 35
Kanchenjunga, Mt 31
Kandahar 31
Kangaroo Island 61
Kano 55
Kanpur 31
Kansas 41
Kansas City 41
Kaohsiung 33
Karachi 31
Karakoram Range 31
Kara Kum Mts 26
Kara Sea 26
Kariba, Lake 59
Karl–Marx-Stadt 19
Karlsruhe 19
Karlstad 13
Kasai river 55
Kashmir see Jammu and Kashmir
Kassel 19
Katmandu 31
Katowice 21
Kattegat 13
Kauai 41
Kawasaki 35
Kazakhstan 27
Kenora 39
Kentucky 41
Kenya 5, 57
Kermadec Islands 63
Kerry, Mts of 9
Khabarovsk 27
Kharkov 26
Khartoum 53
Khyber Pass 31
Kiel 19
Kiel Canal 19
Kiev 26
Kigali 57
Kilimanjaro, Mt 57

Kimberley 59
King Island 61
Kingston 45
Kinshasa 57
Kirgizia 27
Kiribati Republic 63
Kirov 27
Kiruna 13
Kisangani 57
Kishinev 26
Kismaju 57
Kitakyushu 35
Kitwe 59
Klar river 13
Kobe 35
Koblenz 19
Kolyma river 26
Korea see North Korea; South Korea
Kosice 23
Krakatoa 37
Krakow 21
Krefeld 19
Krishna river 31
Kristiansand 13
Kuala Lumpur 37
Kunlun Shan Mts 33
Kunming 33
Kuopio 13
Kuwait 4, 29
Kuwait City 29
Kuybyshev 26
Kyoto 35
Kyushu 35

Laayonne 52
Labrador 39
La Coruna 17
Lagen river 13
Lagos, Nigeria 55
Lagos, Portugal 17
Lahore 31
Lahti 13
Lake District 9
Lanchang Jiang river 33, 37
Land's End 9
Lansing 41
Laos 5, 37
La Paz 47
Lapland 64
La Plata 51
Laptev Sea 26, 64
Las Vegas 40
Latvia 5, 26
Launceston 61
Lausanne 19
Lebanon 4, 29
Leeds 9
Leeward Islands 45
Le Havre 15
Leicester 9
Leichhardt river 61
Leiden 11
Leipzig 19
Lek river 11
Leman, Lake 19
Le Mans 15
Lena river 26
Leon, Mexico 44

Lesotho 5, 59
Lesser Antilles 45
Lesvos 23
Lhasa 33
Liao river 33
Liberia 5, 54
Libreville 55
Libya 5, 53
Liechtenstein 19
Liege 11
Ligurian Sea 25
Lille 15
Lilongwe 59
Lima 47
Limerick 9
Limoges 15
Limpopo river 59
Lincoln 41
Linkoping 13
Linz 19
Lisbon 17
Lithuania 5, 26
Little Rock 41
Liverpool 9
Livorno 25
Ljubljana 23
Ljusnan river 13
Lobito 59
Lodz 21
Lofoten Islands 13
Logan, Mt 38
Loire river 15
Lome 55
Lomond, Loch 9
London 9
Londonderry 9
Long Island 41
Los Angeles 40
Louisiana 41
Louisville 41
Lourdes 15
Lualaba river 57
Luanda 59
Lubeck 19
Lublin 21
Lubumbashi 57
Lucknow 31
Luda see Dalian
Lulea 13
Lule river 13
Luoyang 33
Lusaka 59
Luxembourg 4, 11
Luxor 53
Luzon 37
Lyon 15
Lys river 11

Maas river 11
Maastricht 11
Macao 33
Macdonnell Range 61
Macedonia 23
Maceio 49
Mackenzie Mts 38
Mackenzie river 38–9
Madagascar 5, 59
Madeira 52
Madeira river 47,

49
Madison 41
Madras 31
Madrid 17
Madurai 31
Magdalena river 47
Magdeburg 19
Maggiore, Lake 25
Mahajonja 59
Mahanadi river 31
Maiduguri 55
Maine 41
Main river 19
Mainz 19
Majorca 17
Malabo 55
Malaga 17
Malang 37
Malawi 5, 59
Malawi, Lake see Nyasa, Lake
Malaysia 5, 37
Maldive Islands 5
Mali 4, 52–3
Malmo 13
Malta 25
Man, Isle of 9
Managua 45
Manama 29
Manaus 49
Manchester 9
Manchuria 33
Mandalay 37
Manila 37
Manitoba 39
Mannheim 19
Manukau 63
Maputo 59
Maracaibo 49
Maracaibo, Lake 49
Maranon river 47
Marbella 17
Mar del Plata 51
Mariana Islands 62
Maritsa river 23
Marne river 15
Marquesas Islands 63
Marrakech 52
Marseille 15
Marshall Islands 63
Martinique 45
Maryland 41
Maseru 59
Mashhad 29
Mask, Lough 9
Massachusetts 41
Massif Central 15
Mato Grosso 49
Matsuyama 35
Matterhorn 19
Maui 41
Mauritania 4, 52
Mbabane 59
Mbuji-Mayi 57
Mecca 29
Medan 37
Medellin 47
Medina 29
Mediterranean Sea 15, 17, 23, 25,

29, 52–3
Meerut 31
Mekong see Lanchang Jiang river
Melbourne 61
Melville Island 39, 61
Memphis 41
Mendoza 51
Merida 45
Mesopotamia 29
Messina 25
Metz 15
Meuse river 11, 15
Mexicali 44
Mexico 4, 44–5, 63
Mexico, Gulf of 41, 45
Mexico City 44
Miami 41
Michigan 41
Michigan, Lake 39, 41
Micronesia, Federated States of 63
Middlesborough 9
Midway Islands 63
Milan 25
Milwaukee 41
Mindanao 37
Minneapolis 41
Minnesota 41
Minorca 17
Minsk 26
Miskolc 23
Mississippi 41
Mississippi river 41
Missouri 41
Missouri river 40–1
Mitchell river 61
Miyazaki 35
Moçambique 59
Modena 25
Mogadishu 57
Moldova 26
Molucca Islands 37
Mombasa 57
Monaco 15
Monchen-Gladbach 19
Mongolia 33
Monroe 41
Monrovia 54
Mons 11
Montana 40–1
Montenegro 23
Monterrey 44
Montevideo 51
Montgomery 41
Montpelier, USA 41
Montpellier, France 15
Montreal 39
Morava river 23
Morocco 4, 52
Moscow 27
Mosel river 19
Mosul 29

Map Index

Mount Isa 61
Mozambique 5, 59
Mozambique
  Channel 59
Mulhacen, Mt 17
Mulhouse 15
Munich 19
Munster 19
Murchison river 60
Murcia 17
Murmansk 26, 64
Murray river 61
Murrumbidgee river
  61
Musala, Mt 23
Muscat 29
Musgrave Ranges
  61
Mweru, Lake 59
Myanmar 5, 37
Mykonos 23
Mysore 31

Nagasaki 35
Nagoya 35
Nagpur 31
Nairobi 57
Namib Desert 59
Namibia 5, 59
Namur 11
Nanchang 33
Nancy 15
Nanda Devi 31
Nanjing 33
Nanning 33
Nantes 15
Napier 63
Naples 25
Narbonne 15
Narmada river 31
Narvik 13
Nashville 41
Nassau 45
Nasser, Lake 53
Nauru 63
Naxos 23
N'Djamena 53
Ndola 59
Nebraska 41
Negro river 49, 51
Neisse river 19, 21
Nelson 63
Nelson river 39
Nepal 5, 31
Ness, Loch 9
Netherlands 4, 11
Netze river 21
Nevada 40
Nevis see
  St Kitts-Nevis
Newark 41
New Brunswick 39
New Caledonia 5,
  63
Newcastle 61
Newcastle upon
  Tyne 9
New Delhi 31
Newfoundland 39
New Hampshire 41
New Jersey 41

New Mexico 40-1
New Orleans 41
New Plymouth 63
New Siberian
  Islands 26, 64
New South Wales
  61
New York 41
New York City 41
New Zealand 5, 63
Niagara Falls 39
Niarney 53
Nicaragua 5, 45
Nicaragua, Lake 45
Nice 15
Nicobar Islands 37
Nicosia 29
Niger 4-5, 53
Nigeria 4-5, 55
Niger river 52-3,
  54-5
Niigata 35
Nijmegen 11
Nile river 53
Nimes 15
Nipigon, Lake 39
Nis 23
Norfolk 41
Norrkoping 13
North Africa 4-5,
  52-3
North America 6,
  38-43
North Carolina 41
North Dakota 41
North Downs 9
Northern Ireland 9
Northern Territory
  61
North Korea 5, 33
North Platte river
  40-1
North Pole 64
North Sea 9, 11,
  13, 15, 19
North West
  Highlands 9
Northwest Territories
  38-9
Norway 5, 13
Norwegian Sea 26
Norwich 9
Nottingham 9
Nouakchott 52
Nova Scotia 39
Novaya Zemlya 26,
  64
Novosibirsk 27
Nu Jiang river 33,
  37
Nullarbor Plain
  60-1
Nuremberg 19
Nyasa, Lake 59
Nyiregyhaza 21

Oahu 41
Oakland 40
Oban 9
Ob river 26
Oceania 7, 60-3

Odense 13
Oder river 19, 21
Odessa 26
Offenbach 19
Ohio 41
Ohio river 41
Oise river 15
Okavango Swamps
  59
Okayama 35
Okhotsk, Sea of 26,
  35
Oklahoma 41
Oklahoma City 41
Oldenburg 19
Olympia, Greece
  23
Olympia, USA 40
Olympus, Mt 23
Omaha 41
Oman 5, 29
Omdurman 53
Omsk 27
Ontario 39
Ontario, Lake 39,
  41
Oporto 17
Oran 52
Orange river 59
Ord river 61
Orebro 13
Oregon 40
Orinoco river 49
Orkney Isands 9
Orlando 41
Orleans 15
Osaka 35
Oslo 13
Osorno 51
Ostend 11
Ostrava 23
Ottawa 39
Ouagoudougou 55
Oubangui river 55
Oulu 13
Ouse river 9
Oviedo 17
Oxford 9

Pacific Ocean 6, 7,
  63
Padua 25
Pakistan 5, 31
Palau (trust territory)
  63
Palawan 37
Palembang 37
Palermo 25
Palma 17
Palmer Land 65
Palmerston North 63
Palmyra Islands 63
Pamir Mts 26, 31
Pampas 51
Pamplona 17
Panama 5, 45
Panama Canal 45
Panama City 45
Papua New Guinea
  5, 62
Paraguay 4, 51

Paraguay river 49
Paramaribo 49
Parana river 49, 51
Paris 15
Parma 25
Patagonia 51
Patna 31
Patras 23
Pecs 23
Pembar 57
Pennines 9
Pennsylvania 41
Penzance 9
Perigueux 15
Perm 27
Perpignan 15
Persian Gulf 29
Perth, Australia 60
Perth, Scotland 9
Peru 4, 47
Perugia 25
Philadelphia 5, 37
Philippines 5, 37
Phnom-Penh 37
Phoenix 40
Phoenix Islands 63
Pierre 41
Pindus Mts 23
Piraeus 23
Pisa 25
Pitcairn Island 63
Pittsburgh 41
Piura 47
Platte river 40-1
Ploesti 23
Plovdiv 23
Plymouth 9
Plzen 21
Poland 5, 21
Polar lands 64-5
Pontianak 37
Poona 31
Poopo, Lake 47
Popacatapetl, Mt 44
Pori 13
Po river 25
Port-au-Prince 45
Port Elizabeth 59
Port Harcourt 55
Port Hedland 60
Portland, Maine 41
Portland, Oregon 40
Port Lincoln 61
Port Moresby 62
Porto Alegre 49
Port-of-Spain 49
Porto Novo 55
Portsmouth 9
Port Sudan 53
Portugal 4, 17
Poznan 21
Prague 21
Pretoria 59
Prince Edward Island
  39
Prince George 38
Providence 41
Puebla 44
Pueblo 41
Puerto Montt 51
Puerto Rico 5, 45

Punta Arenas 51
Purus river 49
Pusan 33
Pyongyang 33
Pyrenees 15, 17

Qacentina 53
Qatar 5, 29
Qattara Depression
  53
Qingdao 33
Qiqihar 33
Quebec 39
Queen Elizabeth
  Islands 39, 64
Queen Maud Land
  65
Queensland 61
Quezon City 37
Quito 47

Rabat 52
Raleigh 41
Rangoon 37
Rapid City 41
Ras Dashen, Mt 53
Rawalpindi 31
Reading 9
Recife 49
Red river 40-1
Red Sea 29, 53,
  57
Regensburg 19
Reggio 25
Regina 39
Reims 15
Rennes 15
Reno 40
Revilla Gigedo
  Islands 63
Reykjavik 13, 64
Rhine river 11, 19
Rhode Island 41
Rhodes 23
Rhodope Mts 23
Rhone river 15, 19
Richmond 41
Riga 26
Rijeka 23
Rimini 25
Rio de Janeiro 49
Rio Gallegos 51
Rio Grande river
  40-1, 44-5
Riyadh 29
Rockhampton 61
Rocky Mts 38, 40-1
Romania 5, 23
Rome 25
Roper river 61
Rosario 51
Ross Ice Shelf 65
Ross Sea 65
Rostock 19
Rotorua 63
Rotterdam 11
Roubaix 15
Rouen 15
Rub'al Khali 29
Ruhr river 19
Ruse 23

Russia 26-7
Ruwenzori Range 57
Rwanda 5, 57

Saarbrucken 19
Sabah 37
Sacramento 40
Sacramento river 40
Sahara Desert 52-3
Saint-Etienne 15
St Helens, Mt 40
St John's 39
St Kitts-Nevis 45
St Lawrence river 39
St Louis 41
St Lucia 4, 45
St Paul 41
St Petersburg 26
St Vincent and the
  Grenadines 45
Salado river 51
Salamanca 17
Salem 40
Salerno 25
Salt Lake City 40
Salvador 49
Salween see Nu
  Jiang river
Salzburg 19
Samarkand 27
San'a 29
San Antonio 41
San Diego 40
San Francisco 40
San Joaquin river 40
San Jose, Costa Rica
  45
San Jose, USA 40
San Juan, Argentina
  51
San Juan, Puerto
  Rico 45
San Luis Potosi 44
San Marino 25
San Salvador 45
San Sebastian 17
Santa Clara 45
Santa Cruz 47
Santa Fe, Argentina
  51
Santa Fe, USA 41
Santander 17
Santiago 51
Santiago de
  Compostela 17
Santiago de Cuba
  45
Santo Domingo 45
Santos 49
São Francisco river
  49
Sao Luis 49
Saone river 15
São Paulo 49
São Tomé and
  Principe 55
Sapporo 35
Sarajevo 23
Sarawak 37
Sardinia 25
Saskatchewan 39

Saskatchewan river 39
Saskatoon 39
Sassari 25
Saudi Arabia 5, 29
Sault Ste Marie 39
Savannah 41
Sava river 23
Scandinavia 13
Schelde river 11
Schwerin 19
Scilly Isles 9
Scotland 9
Seattle 40
Segovia 17
Segura river 17
Seine river 15
Semarang 37
Sendai 35
Senegal 5, 54
Senegal river 52, 54
Seoul 33
Serbia 23
Setubal 17
Sevastopol 26
Severnaya Zemlya 26
Severn river 9
Seville 17
Seychelles 5
Sfax 53
Shanghai 33
Shannon river 9
Sheffield 9
Shenyang 33 9
Shetland Islands
Shibelle river 57
Shikoku 35
Shiraz 29
Shizuoka 35
Siberia 27
Sicily 25
Siegen 19
Siena 25
Sierra Leone 5, 54
Sierra Madre del Sur 44–5
Sierra Madre Occidental 44
Sierra Madre Oriental 44–5
Sierra Nevada, Spain 17
Sierra Nevada, USA 40
Sikkim 31
Simpson Desert 61
Singapore 5, 37
Sioux City 41
Skagerrak 13
Skelleftea 13
Skien 13
Skopje 23
Sligo 9
Slovenia 23
Snake river 40
Snowdon 9
Society Islands 63
Sofia 23

Sogne Fiord 13
Solomon Islands 5, 63
Somalia 5, 57
Somme river 15
Songea 57
South Africa 5, 59
South America 6, 46–51
Southampton 9
South Atlantic Ocean 65
South Australia 61
South Carolina 41
South China Sea 33, 35, 37
South Dakota 41
South Downs 9
Southern Alps 63
South Korea 5, 33
South Pacific Ocean 65
South Platte river 40–1
South Pole 65
Southport 61
Spain 4, 17
Sparta 23
Split 23
Spokane 40
Spree river 19
Springfield, Illinois 41
Springfield, Missouri 41
Sri Lanka 5, 31
Srinagar 31
Stavanger 13
Stewart Island 63
Stockholm 13
Stoke-on-Trent 9
Strasbourg 15
Stromboli 25
Stuttgart 19
Sucre 47
Sudan 5, 53
Sudbury 39
Suez 53
Suez Canal 53
Sulawesi 37
Sulu Sea 37
Sumatra 37
Sumba 37
Sumbawa 37
Sundsvall 13
Superior, Lake 39, 41
Surabaya 37
Surakarta 37
Surat 31
Surinam 5, 49
Sutlej river 31
Svalbard 64
Sverdlovsk 27
Swansea 9
Swaziland 5, 59
Sweden 5, 13
Switzerland 4, 19
Sydney 61
Syracuse, USA 41
Syria 4, 29

Szczecin 21
Szeged 23

Tabriz 29
Tadzhikistan 27
Tagus river 17
Taipei 33
Taiwan 5, 33
Taiyuan 33
Talca 51
Tallahassee 41
Tallinn 26
Tampa 41
Tampere 13
Tampico 44
Tana, Lake 53
Tanganyika, Lake 57
Tangier 52
Tangshan 33
Tanzania 5, 57
Tapajos river 49
Taranto 25
Tarim Basin 33
Tarragona 17
Tashkent 27
Tasmania 61
Tasman Sea 61
Taupo, Lake 63
Tay river 9
Tbilisi 26
Tegucigalpa 45
Tehran 29
Tel Aviv-Yafo 29
Temuco 51
Tennant Creek 61
Tennessee 41
Tennessee river 41
Texas 41
Thailand 5, 37
Thailand, Gulf of 33, 37
Thames river 9
Thar Desert 31
Thessaloniki 23
Thimbu 26
Thule 64
Thunder Bay 39
Tianjin 33
Tiber river 25
Tibesti Mts 53
Tibet 33
Tien Shan Mts 26, 33
Tierra del Fuego 51
Tigris river 29
Tijuana 44
Tilburg 11
Timaru 63
Timbuktu 52
Timisoara 23
Timor 37
Timor Sea 37, 60–1
Tirana 23
Tisa river 23
Tisza river 21
Titicaca, Lake 47
Tobago see Trinidad and Tobago
Tocantins river 49
Togo 5, 55

Tokyo 35
Toledo, Spain 17
Toledo, USA 41
Toliara 59
Tomsk 27
Tonga 63
Toowoomba 61
Topeka 41
Torne river 13
Toronto 39
Torrens, Lake 61
Toulon 15
Toulouse 15
Tours 15
Townsville 61
Transylvanian Alps 23
Trenton 41
Trent river 9
Trieste 25
Triglav, Mt 23
Trinidad and Tobago 5, 45, 49
Tripoli 53
Trivandrum 31
Trois Rivieres 39
Tromso 13
Trondheim 13
Trujillo 47
Tsangpao see Brahmaputra river
Tuamotu Islands 63
Tucson 40
Tucuman 51
Tulsa 41
Tunis 53
Tunisia 5, 53
Turin 25
Turkana, Lake 57
Turkey 5, 29
Turkmenistan 26–7
Turku 13
Turnu Severin 23
Tuvalu 63
Tyne river 9
Tyrrhenian Sea 25

Uganda 5, 57
Ujung Pandang 37
Ukraine 26
Ulan Bator 33
Umea 13
Ume river 13
Union of Soviet Socialist Republics, former 5, 26–7, 64
United Arab Emirates 4, 29
United Kingdom 4, 9
United States of America 4, 401
Uppsala 13
Ural Mts 26
Ural river 26
Uruguay 4, 51
Uruguay river 51
Urumqi 33
Utah 40
Utrecht 11

Uzbekistan 26–7

Vaal river 59
Vaasa 13
Valdivia 51
Valencia 17
Valenciennes 15
Valetta 25
Valladolid 17
Valparaiso 51
Vancouver 38
Vancouver Island 38
Vanern, Lake 13
Van river 21
Vanuatu 5, 63
Varanasi 31
Varanger Fiord 13
Vardar river 23
Varna 23
Vasteras 13
Vatican City 25
Vattern, Lake 13
Venezuela 4, 49
Venice 25
Veracruz 45
Vermont 41
Verona 25
Versailles 15
Vesuvius, Mt 25
Victoria, Australia 61
Victoria, Canada 38
Victoria, Lake 57
Victoria Falls 59
Victoria Island 39, 64
Victoria Land 65
Victoria river 61
Vienna 19
Vientiane 37
Vietnam 5, 37
Vigo 17
Vilnius 26
Virginia 41
Vistula river 21
Vladivostok 27
Vltava river 21
Volga river 26
Volgograd 26
Volta, Lake 55
Vosges Mts 15
Vulcano 25

Waal river 11
Waddenzee 11
Wagga Wagga 61
Wakayama 35
Wake Island 63
Wales 9
Wallis and Futuna 63
Walvis Bay 59
Wanganui 63
Wanneroo 60
Warsaw 21
Warta river 21
Washington 40
Washington, DC 41
Waterford 9
Weddell Sea 65
Wellesley Island 61
Wellington 63

Weser river 19
West Africa 54–5
West Bank 29
Western Australia 60–1
Western Ghats 31
Western Sahara 52
Western Samoa 63
West Virginia 41
Whitehorse 38
White Nile river 53
Whyalla 61
Wichita 41
Wicklow Mts 9
Wiesbaden 19
Wight, Isle of 9
Wilkes Land 65
Windhoek 59
Winnipeg 39
Winnipeg, Lake 39
Wisconsin 41
Wollongong 61
Wroclaw 21
Wuhan 33
Wuppertal 19
Wurzburg 19
Wyoming 40–1

Xi'an 33
Xi-Jiang river 33
Xingu river 49
Xuzhou 33

Yangtze see Chang Jiang river
Yaounde 55
Yellowknife 38
Yellow Sea 33
Yemen 5, 29
Yenisey river 26
Yerevan 26
Yichang 33
Yokohama 35
York 9
Yucatan Peninsula 45
Yugoslavia 4, 23
Yukon river 38
Yukon Territory 38

Zagreb 23
Zagros Mts 29
Zaire 5, 57
Zaire river 55
Zambezi river 59
Zambia 5, 59
Zanzibar 57
Zaragoza 17
Zhengzhou 33
Zimbabwe 5, 59
Zurich 19

General Index

Page numbers in *italics* refer to illustration captions.

Aborigines 60
Adriatic Sea 22
Alps 14, 18, *18*
Aluminium 60
Amazon Basin 46, 48, 75
Amsterdam *10*
Amundsen, Roald 65
Andes Mts *46*, *50*
Andros 23
Antarctica 50, 65, *65*
Apartheid 58
Apennine Mts 24
Arctic 64
Aswan High Dam 52
Atacama Desert 50
Atlas Mts 52
Auckland 62
Ayers Rock *61*

Baltic Sea 20
Baltic States 26
Bananas 46, 62
Barley 20, 26
Berber people 52, *52*
Bougainville 62
Brahmaputra river 30
Brussels *10*
Budapest 20
Buddhism *35*, 36, *37*
Buenos Aires *50*

Caracas 48
Caribbean 45, *45*
Carpathian Mts 20
Cassava 54, 56
Cattle 20, 40, 50, 54, 56, *56*, 58, 60, 62
Chang Jiang river 32
Chemical industries 18
Chicago 42
Christianity *14*, 16, 24, 28, 48
Citrus fruit 16, 24 see also Fruit
Coal mining 20, 22, 26, 42, 48
Cocoa 54, 56, 62
Coconuts 62
Coffee 36, 44, 46, 48, 54, 56
Columbus, Christopher

44
Commonwealth of Independent States 26
Communism 20, 26, 32
Cook, Captain James 60
Copper 22, 50, 56, 60, 62
Coral reefs *62*
Cork 16
Cotton 40, 44, 50, 54, 56, 58
Couscous *55*
Croats 22

Dairy farming 10, 12, 14, 26, 62
Dams 18, 52
Danube river 20
Deserts 28, *28*, 32, 52, 52, 58, 60, 75
Diamonds 58
Djibouti 56

Earthquakes 34
Electrical and electronics industries 10, 18, 34, *34*
Equator 46
Everest, Mt 30, 75

Fiords 12
Fishing 8, 12, 16, 34, 38, 62, 64
Flower growing 10
Food processing industries 12, 16
Forests 12, *12*, 22, 36, 38, 46, 48, 54, 56
Fruit 14, 18, 22, 44, 46, *46* see also Citrus fruit
Fuji, Mt 34

Game reserves 56, *58*
Ganges river 30
Geysers 12
Goats *10*, 22
Gold 44, 58, *58*, 60, 62
Grasslands 50, 54, 56
Great Lakes 42, 75
Greek islands 22
Greeks, Ancient 22
Greenland 12

Hadramaut (Yemen) *28*

Herding 32, 54, 56, *56*, 64
Himalayas 30, *30*
Hindu religion 30
Hong Kong *32*
Hot springs 12
Huang He river 32
Hudson Bay 38
Hunters 56, 64
Hydroelectricity 18

Iguaçu Falls 48
Inca people 46, *46*
Indians, American 38, 40, 44, 46, 48
Indus river 30
Inuit (Eskimos) 38, 64
Iron 10, 12, 32, 48, 60
Irrigation 16, 28
Islam 28, 30, 36, 52

Jerusalem 28
Jewish people 28
Jura Mts 14

Kalahari Desert 58
Kenya, Mt 56

Lapps 64, *64*
Li river valley (China) 32
Lisbon 16
Los Angeles 42
Lyon 14

Machu Picchu *46*
Maize 44, 54, 56, 58
Mangrove swamps *45*
Maori people 62
Mao Zedong 32
Marseille 14
Masai tribe 58
Mayan civilisation 44
Mecca 28
Medina 28
Melanesia 62
Micronesia 62
Milan 24
Millet 54, 56
Mining 20, 22, 26, 36, 42, 44, 46, 50, 54, 56, 58, 58, 60
Monsoons 30
Mont Blanc 14
Monument Valley, USA 42
Moscow 27
Motor vehicle industry

18, *18*, 24, 50, 54
Muslims see Islam

Naples 24
Natural Gas 10, 26, 42, 50
Nauru 62
New York City *40*
Nile river 52, 75
Nitrates 50

Oases 28, 52
Oil 8, 10, 22, 26, 28, *28*, 36, 42, 44, 48, 50, 54
Olives 16, 24

Pacific Islands 62, *62*
Palm oil 54, 56
Pamir Mts 26
Pampas 50
Paper manufacture 12
Paris 14, *14*
Persian Gulf 28
Phosphates 62
Plantains 56
Plastics industry 50
Plateaus 16, 32, 46, 56, 58
Polders 10
Polynesia 62
Potatoes 16, 20, *20*
Prairies 38
Pyramids 52
Pyrenees 14, 16

Rhine river 18
Rice 16, 34, 36
Rocky Mts 39, *40*, 42
Roman Catholic Church 24, 48
Rome 24
Rubber 36, *36*, 54, 56
Rye 20, 26

Sacre Coeur *14*
Sahara Desert 52, *52*
Santa Maria della Salute 24
Santiago 50
Savanna grasslands 54, 56
Serbs 22
Sheep 22, *40*, 50, 60, 62, 62
Shinto religion *35*
Shipbuilding 20, 34

18, *18*, 24, 50, 54
Sierra Nevada 16
Silver 60
Sports 18, *42*
Steel 10, 32, 50
Sugar beet 14, 20
Sugar cane 44, 48, 50
Sydney Opera House 60

Taj Mahal *30*
Tea *30*, 56
Temples 34, *35*, *37*
Textiles 10, 16, 24, 54
Tierra del Fuego 50
Tin mining 36, 46
Tobacco 36, 40, 44, 58
Tourism 14, 16, 22, 24, *24*, 44, 52, 56
Turin 24
Tuscany 24

Ural Mts 26

Vancouver *38*
Vatican City 24
Venice 24
Vesuvius, Mt 24
Volcanoes 12, 24, 34, *34*, 36
Vosges Mts 14

West Indies 44
Wheat 16, 20, *20*, 26, 38, 50
Wildlife 22, 56, 58, *58*
Wine 14, *14*, 16, 22, 24

Yams 54, 56

Zaire river 56, 75
Zinc 22, 60

ACKNOWLEDGEMENTS

The publishers wish to thank the following for supplying photographs for this book:

Page 1 ZEFA; 8 ZEFA; 10 ZEFA; 12 Dave Saunders (top) ZEFA (bottom); 14 ZEFA (top) Helene Rogers (bottom); 16 TRIP/Life File; 17 ZEFA; 18 ZEFA; 20 ZEFA; 22 ZEFA; 23 The Hutchison Library; 24 ZEFA; 26 ZEFA; 27 ZEFA; 28 ZEFA; 30 Helene Rogers (top) ZEFA (bottom); 31 TRIP/Life File; 32 ZEFA; 33 Eye Ubiquitous; 34 ZEFA; 35 TRIP/Life File; 36 ZEFA; 37 ZEFA; 38 ZEFA; 39 ZEFA; 40 Helene Rogers (top) Grant Heilman (bottom); 42 ZEFA; 44 Lally St.Maur; 45 Helene Rogers; 50 ZEFA (top) Eye Ubiquitous (bottom); 52 Helene Rogers; 53 Eye Ubiquitous; 54 Eye Ubiquitous (left) TRIP/Life File (right); 55 TRIP/ Clive Farndon; 56 Eye Ubiquitous; 57 The Hutchison Library; 58 ZEFA; 59 Dave Saunders; 60 ZEFA; 62 TRIP/ Joan Wakelin (left) ZEFA (right); 64 Finnish Tourist Office; 65 TRIP/Norman Price.

Picture Research: Su Alexander and Elaine Willis